Thresholds & Archways

Thresholds & Archways

One Christian's Collection
Prayers, Poems & Perspectives

Victor Murray

Copyright © 2004 by Victor Murray
ISBN: 1-4134-4041-X

All rights reserved. No part of this book may be reproduced or transmitted in any form or by any means, electronic or mechanical, including photocopying, recording, or by any information storage and retrieval system, without permission in writing from the author.

This book was printed in the United States of America.

Contents

Thresholds & Archways	13
Salvation's Rain	15
The Seeds In The Core	17
The Tools of a Carpenter	18
Eden	19
Wondrous Morning	21
Nature's Stewards	22
A Labor of Love	24
The Blacksmith's Hammer	26
The Music of Life	28
May I See You One More Time	29
Gentle Whispers & Tumultuous Thunder	30
A Once Proud Man	31
Memories	32
Do You Count Your Blessings	33
A Christmas Prayer	35
Beseech Me This	36
Faithfully They Gather	37
A Mother of Nature	38
The Light from Within	39
The Crescent Moon	41
The Spillway of Faith	42
The Chill Before Dawn	45
In the Eyes of a Child	47
Before the Bud Opens	48
Out of the Mist of Histories Past	49
The Indigo Bunting	50
Where No Wood Is, There The Fire Goes Out	52
Disciples	53
Hosanna	55
Of All the Senses	57

OUT OF THE WOODS	60
HOW GRACIOUS IS HE	61
OH LORD	62
PRIORITIES	63
THE EVENING'S CALM	64
THROUGH CRESTING WAVES	65
COMPASSION	66
ONE LIFE IS BUT THE COST	67
THE BLESSINGS OF DIVERSITY	68
CLOSER THAN ONE KNOWS	69
WHEN ALL THAT ONE HAS	70
DEAR LORD	71
REFLECTIONS	72
HIS IS THE LIGHT	74
ALL IN GOOD TIME	75
HOW PLENTIFUL THE HARVEST	76
LOVING KINDNESS AND TENDER MERCIES	77
WHAT DOES HE SEE	78
THE BENCH IN MY GARDEN	79
THE DOG DAYS OF SUMMER	81
BY BREAD ALONE	83
THE MASTER BUILDER	84
GRACE & UNDERSTANDING	85
THE TWILIGHT	86
THE TWILIGHTS OF MANKIND	88
WISDOM AND UNDERSTANDING	89
CHILDREN'S CHILDREN	90
WITH ONE OPTION LEFT	91
ON A MISSION OF TRUTH	92
AT THE FOOT OF HIS THRONE	93
THE GARDEN OF PEACE	94
BUT ONE FREEDOM	95
IN THE GATHERING OF FAITH	96
THE NORTH STAR	97
THE WINDS OF CHANGE	98
THE HALF MAST	100
WHAT DOES IT MEAN TO BE AMERICAN?	101
IN THE GATHERING	102

A Senseless Act	103
Blessed is the Gathering	104
Look into Their Windows	106
A Ship	108
The Song of Calvary	110
One Leaf of All	111
For Lynne	113
A Way Back Home	115
When My Savior Comes for Me	117
To Judge Thee Not Guilty	118
Wisdom	119
Romancing The Stars	120
A Village Thanksgiving	122
A Way Back Home	123
A Need Unknown	125
A Place of Prayer, Pride and Purpose	127
The "I" Beam of Democracy	130
The Christmas Gift	132
A Manger in Your Heart	133
Forgive Us Our Debts	134
Among the Faithful in the Followers	136
In One's Best Interest	138
A Journey Within	140
The Vision We Seek	142
The Endless Gift	143
There is a Peace to be Found	144
Partakers of Grace	145
The Threshold of Compassion	147
The Limit of One's Horizon	149
St. Paul's Trinity Church	150
The Tracks We Leave and Follow	152
They Knew Him Not	154
A Prayer for the Weary	155
The Ritual of Recovery	156
A Morning Prayer	158
The Mile and the Mill Stones	159
Through the Garden Gate One Enters By His Way	161
To Thine Own Self Be True	163

THE GOOD MORNING	164
THE GOLDEN SPIRIT MIRACLE	166
MEMORIAL DAY	167
THE MESSENGER OF THE COVENANT	168
SUFFICE FOR THE DAY	170
A BLESSING IN HIS SIGHT	171
THE BURDEN OF MY YOKE	172
PREPARING FOR THY SEED	174
THE DESIRES OF MAN AND THE GLORY OF HEAVEN	176
TARRY NOT	178
THE POTTER'S FIELD	179
THE FIREWORKS OF FREEDOM	180
A PLAN FOR PEACE	182
THE BORDER OF HIS GARMENT	184
A WONDER TO BEHOLD	186
AND FOLLOWED JESUS "IN THE WAY"	188
THERE BUT FOR THE GRACE	190
THE WORD OF GOD UNTO . . .	191
AND HIS MOTHER SHALL KEEP	192
CLARITY OF PURPOSE	194
DREAMS THAT MEMORIES MAKE	196
INSIGHT	197
THE CIRCLES OF FAITH	199
THE FIRST STAR OF THE EVENING	201
". . . AND WHEN THOU ART CONVERTED, STRENGTHEN THY BRETHERAN."	202
DECISIONS	204
A YEAR OF REFLECTION	206
ABIDETH NOT ALONE	208
SEE IT THROUGH	210
NOT KNOWING THE FATHER	212
A NEW WINE	213
AN EVEN TIDE	215
UNBRIDLED LOYALTY	216
A CHARIOT OF FAITH	218
THY WILL BE DONE	220
WHAT MEASURE	221
THE APPRECIATION DEFICIT	222
THE PRISONER WITHIN	223

For None are the Risen	225
The Fig and the Folly	227
The Praises of Charity	229
Whose Will Be Done	231
The Greatest Power	233
God is True	235
How We are Known	237
Survival and The Word of "One God"	239
The Image We Leave	241
"I Do Not Frustrate the Grace of God . . ."	243
Sedona	245
Your Christian Faith	247
What He Wants	248
Dear Lord	250
Halos	252
Of Those Who Have Come to Greet . . .	254
Greetings	256
When Worlds Collide	258
Walk Worthy of God	261
For God so ever loved the world	263
Some Years the Christmas Message	265
The Bible on My Pen	267
Forever	268
The "-ations" of our Worlds	269
Oh Where the Works of Wright	271
According to the Gospel	272
This Day	274
Fight Your Fears	275
Time	276
Hebrews 9—Perfection of Christ's Sacrifice	277
By thy Hand	279
The Second Snowfall	280
Columbia A Blessed Mission	282
Land of Milk & Honey	283
Burl Wood	284
Beyond and Within	285
Ports of Unity	287
Eve and Mourn	289

Noah	291
A Compassionate Lot	293
The Watershed	294
Reminders	296
The Blessings of the Son	298
The Love in One's Land	300
It Is	302
The Bee Line Prayer	303
Traditions	305
The Garden Path	307
Through Visions Clear	309
In The Company of Strangers	310
Pilate & Herod The Validation Sought	312
Where We Will Find	314
Dear Lord,	315
Saviour (Savior)	316
Remember Your Baptism	317
All Honor, Praise and Glory	318
A Warrior's Lament	320
Blessed Assurance	321
When Thou Shalt Harken	322
Before the Cock Crows	323
In the Midst of His Temple	325
A City of Truth	326
De"scribing" the Naysayer	327
The Surety of the Shoe	329
The Prayers of Thy Servants	331
God's Call to Repentance	333
Mist of Mine Eyes	336
In Search of Peace	337
A Pioneer's Prayer	338
Duty & The Golden Rule	339
The Shittim Wood	340
Always on Watch	341
Hide & Seek	343
Trailings	345
Liberty	347
Seeing It Through, II	348

A CHILD OF GOD, AND CHILDREN OF HIS WORKS	350
FOR THOSE LOW IN SPIRIT	352
COMPANIONS AND CHRIST	353
HERO IN THE HEART	355
FILLED WITH PRAYERS AND WISHES	356
THE SEAL IS BROKEN . . . BUT THE CONTENTS ARE SAFE	357
PEACE ON EARTH	359
A FAITHFUL CROSSING	360

Thresholds & Archways

One of the most beautiful features of churches and institutions of higher learning is the gothic archway. A classic merger of "form and function" the gothic archway combines both the natural strength of stone with the power of attentive human creativity.

At the peak of many doorways, a single keystone can be found; but in a lancet arch one can find two key stones, where the assembled pressures from opposing sides come together. As with the original stonecutter, this is where one can often find their faith. A point where that which we question, and that which we trust within our hearts, must come together before we move on; for even at the pinnacle of life, there is still a threshold yet to be crossed.

In the academic world it is often a special teacher who helps you discover your talent and that hidden passion you never knew you possessed. In faith it is frequently that personal struggle that bears down on you, barring you from moving forward, until you discover the strength from the One above you, who protects you from all sides.

My public education and spiritual enlightenment can be found through two such archways in my life, to who I dedicate this book.

At the educational threshold, I recall my seventh grade English teacher, Mrs. Carlton. A kind, yet firm disciplinarian, her soft voice forced us all to strain our attention on each and every word and lesson. This technique required our asking to have some points repeated and encouraged after-class discussions to stay on course with the lessons of the day.

It is not often that one is blessed with their discovery of faith to one particular moment or event in their life. For me, however, it was on the morning of March 8, 1998, at the grave of my brother. The events of a lifetime of brotherhood, and the blessed gift of salvation were reaffirmed in a story that came together that day, and is recounted herein.

To begin this journey of discovery, this collection of poems, prayers and perspectives is dedicated to Mrs. Carlton, and my brother, Scott Jeffrey Murray. I hope that this collection will help the reader discover where their passions can be found, and reaffirm their faith in the Lord and the everlasting love of our Savior, Jesus Christ. For the keystones of life are our faith in the Lord and the love of our Savior, above each and every archway to be crossed.

Salvation's Rain

Just days before my brother died,
    I watched him sleep at his bedside.
He awoke, reached out and held my hand,
    and whispered these words to understand.

He said "We sail on different ships."
    And as our hands did tightly grip,
I replied "The sails that we had set
    will bring us back to where we met."

As he fell back asleep and I arose to my feet,
    there came a voice I could barely hear.
I turned around and there I found,
    a solemn face, with an awful fear.

He looked at my pity, asking "Did I live in the city?"
    He said "It is a dark and dangerous place."
As my answer was "no" there came back a glow,
    and a smile across his face.

His smile was sweet, as our eyes did meet
    in ways of understanding.
Before too long, with God's winds so strong,
    it was his that would be the first landing.

Ten years to the day that Scott had died,
    I greeted the day at his graveside.
With fearful thoughts "Had he been saved?"
    I opened my Bible to this sweet page.
It was Matthew nine; verse one that I would read,
    the words of salvation we both would need.

"And he entered *a ship* and passed over, *and came into **his own city**. And, behold, they brought to him a man sick of the palsy, lying on a bed: and Jesus seeing their faith said unto the sick of the palsy: *Son, be of good cheer;* **thy sins be forgiven thee.**"

A year later, as I drove up to Scott's grave, two speckled fawns ran on ahead of me; jumping gracefully over the gravestones on both sides of the road, they crisscrossed in front of my car. As I reached the top of the hill, one disappeared in the fog; the other stopped, quietly watched me. As I passed by, I looked back and there by the fawn the fog lifted, and the name on the gravestone, "SCOTT," appeared.

On March 8, 1998, the lessons of the scriptures touched my heart as my tears met the pages of Matthew 9. Mixed with a light rain that began at the opening of the first verse, by the end of my reading on that day of Lent, the rain had stopped and a burden that I had carried was lifted from my shoulders.

On August 21, 1999 (the day before what would have been my brother's 47th birthday) Christ's conquest over the grave was confirmed with an innocent vision of nature's joy through two young fawns.

May the Glory of Life Everlasting through Jesus Christ be remembered in our hearts, now and forever.

The Seeds In The Core

Every tree that bears fruit has a majesty all its own. In the spring the blossoms fill the orchards with a sweet aroma, pleasing colors to the eye and songbirds sound the arrival of a new season's promise. As summer nears, the bees give way and yield to the fruits that announce that life will prevail. In the fall, vibrancy abounds in a multitude of color, and the leaves crackle under foot, as the orchard is prepared for the long winter slumber.

Long after the apples have been harvested and prepared for consumption or storage, nature preserves what man often discards . . . the seeds in the core.

In the early morning calm, in a home at the end of the road, a mother rises with the sun and quietly prepares a meal for the family's busy day. The children roll in their beds as their father calls out their names in a scratchy morning voice. Outside the cool morning air moves sheets of mist off the warming water of the lake. The sun's rays break over the knoll on the pasture, announcing the dawning of a new day. Unaware that this young boy's dawn will one day be a welcomed visitor to an old man's memories.

As we struggle to tend the fruit that we have frantically sown and carefully watched over, it is important to take the time to reflect on the seeds in the core. Like the old apple tree that has gnarled and bent under the strain of responsibility and weathered the worries of many winters, today's man needs to take heart in the seeds in the core of his soul, and let God preserve what man discards.

The Tools of a Carpenter

TRUTH
Like the wood plane that shaves away chips of hardwood, the smooth grains of a finely finished surface are revealed in time. God sent to us a young carpenter, centuries ago. Through his words and teachings we can shed years of guilt and confusion to expose the truth of our very being.

LOVE
The hardest woods give way to the many honed teeth of a carpenter's saw. Love brings us together, and together our love cuts through life's greatest challenges.

COMPASSION
The hammer's strike requires a keen eye, a steady hand and a strong Will. Compassionate people see problems clearly, take hold of the situation firmly, and relentlessly pursue until a solution can be found.

FAITH
The toolbox of a carpenter is where one assembles all of one's tools together, not to rest, but to be carried wherever they are needed. Faith brings God's tools together; it carries us in times of fixing past mistakes, repairing current problems and building new dreams.

This Christmas, I received another tool from my son. Every year I look forward to these gifts. And every year my toolbox grows. With God's help, may His tools be put to good use.

December 31, 1997

Eden

Can you hear the silence? Will you find the peace? Can one loose what is never lost? Can one become deaf to one's own soul?

Eden. Is it a place from the past . . . Never to be found again? Or a present brought with Christ, waiting to be opened. It is here. It is everywhere, every second of every minute; before everyone's eyes, yet hidden from many hearts. It is what binds us all; one with the same sweet air that fills our lungs. One with the skies that welcome the sun when we rise, and embraces distant stars while we rest.

Peace is a song. Sung by a soft winter's breeze in thick mountain pines; cooed by an infant held in their mother's cradling arms and harmonized on the wings of passing geese. While wave's pound a steady beat on our rocky cliffs of dreams.
Christ showed us that these are not the things of dreams. When He threw out the money changers at the temple's entrance, was it a sign of man's reality? A sinful man's reality clutters the steps to the natural order. Every day we set up tables for the day's work before us. With our backs to the temple, we seek the attention of those passing before us. Looking down the steps toward man's reality we are blind to the Truth that awaits us when our last sun has set.

I believe that Eden is still here. Through Jesus Christ our Lord, God showed us that He has always been here in the Eden that He created. But when Jesus left us, he left us with so much more. As soldiers gambled over the only possession that He owned, His robe, so has man bartered over all that we have created. But Jesus left us with much more. For as His words opened the eyes of the blind, and as His hands brought sound to the deaf, so does His life invite us to see the beauty and hear the sounds of Eden.

For it was man who chose to not heed God's word; but it was our Lord's compassion, for our self imposed plight, that sent us a Savior in Christ Jesus.

This Christmas season, I am most thankful for the gift of life: a life in the Eden that is still here. An eternal life in Christ Jesus our Savior.

January 4, 1998

Wondrous Morning

What a wondrous morning. The sounds of falling water set the tone as songbirds greet the new day. Stillness is in the air allowing one to rise from a deep sleep with ease, and a welcomed spirit is born again. Truly the Lord's mercy can be felt when a new day begins; when the trials and tribulations of a day now past . . . retreat from the light of a new.

In the second book of Samuel, Chapter 23, Verse 4 it is written: *"And he shall be as the light of the morning, when the sun riseth, even a morning without clouds, as the tender grass springing out of the earth by clear shining after rain."*

On this morning, that one special morning in one's life, may we welcome our Savior into our hearts. May the words of the bible speak to those who seek to lead in these days of campaigning now before us. For it is written:

*"The God of Israel said, the Rock of Israel spake to me, He that ruleth over men **must** be just, ruling in the fear of God."*

May the spirit of the Lord speak through those who seek to lead, and may His words be in their tongue.

Selah

July 29, 2000

Nature's Stewards

The gentle fall breeze picks up in response the retreating sun. In the distance a lone cricket sounds its chirps in search of a mate . . . a sound that is unlikely to be answered. This s the time to rest and reflect on the day's long labors. The Lord has seen to it that the billowing clouds passing overhead hold off on their appointed round of rain.

As one of nature's stewards, I welcome the sight of my sweet wife in her quest to see that the gardens are top-dressed with mulch. The young trees and recently transplanted scrubs welcome the warm, steaming mulch as it rises through the crisp, dry leaves. Our work arouses a mole who darts in through the myrtle, preparing for the first frost which announces the rapidly approaching winter season.

No matter what tasks fail to be completed near day's end, our weary muscles beckon us to lay down our tools. It will not be long before we enjoy the warmth of a roaring fire above the stone hearth. As the rich aroma of a burning mulberry log will soon fill the house, my thoughts will then drift back to many family memories that will bring warmth to the soul.

But for now, it is time to give up the day and welcome the night, as a bear welcomes its well-earned winter slumber. It is time; time to reflect on pleasures of creation. How God's mighty hands made flesh out of dust, and with a single breath brought life anew.

Every Fall I enjoy the brisk winds and crisp air. It restores my soul and stirs me into what new wonders the winter will bring. Longing for our new-found family hobby, we look forward to the first light snow, and the chance to break out our cross-country skis.

Trekking out upon the crisp winter snow,
I welcome the trails that we choose to go.
On gliding ski's we pass on through time
A special journey, that is yours, and is mine.

One sets the path for the others to follow
And leads us on, over hills and through hollows
The crisp hard snow yields to the first active ski,
As we glide on behind, almost effortlessly.

We know how far to go before stopping
To return back home, we turn and, start hopping
Back on the path that God's blessing has set
We journey back home to where we first met

No matter how far we choose to roam,
The path set by Christ will soon bring us home.

October 8, 2000

A Labor of Love

A labor of love before the break of day
He ventures out to give cattle their hay
Lots to do, and little to say
This is the life, the farmer's way.

The fields are furrowed the windmills spin
Both efforts uncover the strength found within
One feeds the roots, one captures the wind
Our Lord's assurance that the good life will win

A bounty will follow and food will abound
With patience and caring will come from the ground
A harvest of plenty, a feast to be found
A faith in the future, with nary a sound
The blessings of Jesus were sewn long ago
The disciples of Jesus today truly know
That with faith and thanksgiving His pure love will grow
Praise His words and His teachings, wherever they go

The greatest of creations that life has to offer is itself, "life." This may sound a little odd at first, but think about it for minute. In today's complex and ever demanding world, our senses are constantly bombarded with sights, sounds, images and messages of what is supposed to be important to us. We have telephones, television, faxes, e-mails, Internet and Intranets (no, I didn't stutter, it's a little semantics thing).

There was a time when we had to go to these sources of communication, but today, not are they everywhere, but now they travel with us. Like this portable PC, that I carry to record my thoughts. More than a recording devise; it is a "complete" handheld computer with spreadsheets, word processor, voice recording, e-mail capabilities, and electronic book (where I can download entire books) and it can even communicate with my PC and other peoples' handheld PDA's via infrared signal. This thing is so smart it can even read my handwriting . . . I can't even do that! Believe it or not . . . they are now developing computers that you can wear. I guess "double breasted will soon mean your Armani comes in stereo!

On "World Communion Day" just two weeks ago I wrote of the images that flashed across the screens of a young child and man caught in the crossfire. Moments later the child slumped against the man who was frantically waving to warn of their defenseless position. A few seconds later, he followed the child in their shared journey" Last night I came home to similar images from the Middle East. But this time there were crowds, rocket fire and a gapping hole in a war ship. Here many brave Americans had died in cowardly act of terrorism.'

Men reap what men sow. Where are the fields of wheat and peace to be found in such a world? The false sense of "power" as the ability to destroy has been created through images. What of the power to live and to grow?

If the greatest of creations that life has to offer is itself, life; then, maybe the worst of creations that life has to offer is the taking of itself. Centuries ago a child came into our lives to lead us to peace. His death on the cross as a young man has become our symbol of salvation. I knew that some would use the image of this young child dying in the crossfire to lead them to war. They will sow the seeds of violence and in so doing shall reap their own destruction.

Now six or more of our own join them; caught in the crossfire. What we do, now . . . now with our own images. A child came into our lives to show us the way to peace.

October 13, 2000

The Blacksmith's Hammer

The blacksmith's hammer strikes hard and true. A keen eye and steady hand will see it through. Out of the dark coal and the embers' red glow, fiery hot steel will soon come to show: the way out of darkness is not an easy task, especially if one is too proud to ask. Our Lord is there to show us the way, and guide us out to the light of day.

I was born in Pittsburgh; well, technically Homestead Hospital. This small steel mill town located on the Monongahela River was not only known for its steel manufacturing prowess, but in the history books, Homestead may well have been the birthplace of the American Steel Workers Union movement. Here is where one of our nation's greatest conflicts arose between steel workers, the management and the Federal government: this was where the Homestead Riots occurred.

I've always believed that the strongest steel is forged in the hottest of fires. The human spirit never ceases to amaze me. Catastrophic events in one's life hold the promise to destroy or resurrect one's self. This is especially true for many Americans who share a special place in history. Rebellion, conflict and reunification have always been the catalyst for dramatic changes in our society.

As we continue an unprecedented period of peace and prosperity, many will take credit for these times, while pointing out the pitfalls that lay ahead. In an election year, when candidates frantically search for differences that can set themselves apart, the seeds of discourse are already being sown.

Before the winter of our economy begins,
The politicians and pun dents will weave a new spin.

They will praise their actions and discredit the others,
While kissing the babies and wooing the mothers

For little is lost when it comes to digress,
Better to avoid the issues, than to answer the press.

These are the days when they ask us to vote,
So when they're elected, there's a reason to gloat:

How the two party system is the best that can be,
When I give one to you, you owe one (maybe, two) to me?

For all of the problems and all that we suffer,
A free election is still the best that this world has to offer.

The Music of Life

The music of life is a sweet, soft song
The melody and tune going on and on
He knows all its beats and counts all its measures
God sets all the lows and the highs that we treasure.

Then together we gather, the song sung on key
That's when the music or life means the most to me.

May I See You One More Time

May I see you one more time?
And let us speak as friends.
May I see you one more time?
The sweetness never ends.
We've shared a kinship built on love
The greatest power in life
We've shared the good times and the sad
My friend, my love, my wife
When feeling low, you've picked me up
And stood me on my feet
When feeling high, you've brought me back
Humble and so sweet

The sun may set but once each day
But by God's holy grace,
The sun will rise, as in your eyes,
And bring warmth upon my face.

Fear not the years that come and go
And cherish every moment
Bear not the tears, and welcome years
Our wondrous days will come again
And time will be well spent.

May you see me one more time?
On that you can depend.
May you see me anytime?
Our love will never end.

Gentle Whispers &

Tumultuous Thunder

Lightly, delicately the fingers weave their magic
Be it sweet, soft dreams or a life so tragic . . .
Over strings, across bows,
Guiding wind through a reed flows

A sound so soft and sweet,
The symphony leads, our fears retreat
The drums pound out a hastening pace
As violins join in the wonderful race.

Of sights and sounds that stir the soul
The maestro's hands need not consol
Be, it a gentle whisper or tumultuous thunder
The orchestra sets our souls asunder

November 15, 2000

How can one capture in words what shakes the very soul when watching a great performance? It could be a star athlete spiraling over a high bar, or a stirring orator caught in an historical moment. Sometimes we are blessed with such great experiences that bring together many wonderful skills and artistry, like watching a ballet or listening to a musical.

While watching the Philadelphia Philharmonic's 100th Anniversary performance on PBS, I was captivated by the sights and sounds that emanated before me.

A Once Proud Man

A once proud man will make amends
With others all around
Once faced with facts salvation sends
A truth of life is found.

When friends fore sake and sons equate
you with yesterday's once proud story.
Reaching back in time to what once was mine,
a sense of fame and glory.

For when getting old, one not so bold
And reality is not quite lost
We'll take back the day, when we're content to say:
The journey was worth the cost.

November 21, 2000

A once proud man leaves his memories in his footprints
Lets the sands of time wash away his trouble and his pain
Never regretting the choices that he didn't make
Leaves to those what others take
The world he leaves behind

When pain and sorrow are greater than the joy we feel
Of what are lies and what is real
When no longer can one live a lie
A once proud life is left to die

Memories

They glisten like one billion diamonds
Scattered across a lake of blue
Drifting with the winds and currents
Beckoning out to me and to you.

The gulls glide by underneath a sky
Where geese find their fall formation
Squirrels give way and begin to play
While others begin a long hibernation.

When the winter winds blow and one comes to know
Of the wonder of their own creation
That is when Peace of mind takes over in time
As one awakens to their own salvation.

The glistening gives way to the cold morning frosts
As the days grow short with 'pleasure
The days that are lost are worth twice the cost
With these memories that I've come to treasure.

November 24, 2000

Do You Count Your Blessings

Do you count your blessings?'
Do they sound all right?
Do they number many,
And keep you warm at night?

For when you're feeling hunger
And have food right at your hand
Do you give a blessing?
And begin to understand:

That for all, life is a miracle.
We depend on God's pure grace.
When facing needs of others.
There can be no hiding place.

The hunger is a yearning.
For what we truly need
And it cannot be fulfilled
By excess, or wanton greed.

Yes, blessings should be counted
But not by counts or measure
the blessings of our sharing
Is what we all should treasure.

December 2, 2000

Events of the past few days strike deep into my sense of self worth. I have felt low in spirit, weak in faith and somewhat out of touch with my own values. A disappointment with others has probably masked a disappointment in me, as I came to recognize a feeling that has been foreign to me for most of my life: resentment. Why? I do not know. But when I received a daily inspire message, today it read: "Resentment is drinking poison and waiting for the other person to die."

Although my message came through an e-mail, messages can come in many forms. Often we interpret long bouts of silence with fear and suspicion. Counting how many times one is called, or how many times one calls others, can become very self demeaning. What should be counted as a blessing is the fact that you care and have others that you care about; this is one of life's greatest blessings. But resentment can set in if you "count" the number of calls rather than the blessing that you have someone to call.

This importance of this message could not have been more clearly made than when I returned a call from my younger brother this week. After being a little perturbed for having left two unanswered messages for him over the past two weeks, I looked forward to his voice, but not the news that he had to deliver.

For what ever time we share on this earth, there' a reassurance that sweeps over us when we hear the voice of those we love. It reminds us of who we are that we are not alone and that someone else cares.

Before us all . . . there was love

A Christmas Prayer

He awoke to a world of wonder
In a manger far away
The King of kings, our Savior
On a bed of Christmas hay.

The shepherds led processions
As angels herald on high
They came from distant places
By a special starlit sky

The camels crossed the desert
As lambs and lions lay.
The pilgrimage they followed
Continues through this day.

'With gifts we honor His arrival
As kings did long ago
We follow their special welcome
And prepare our lives to show:

That a world can welcome Christmas
With a quiet, yet joyful, psalm
It takes but sweet salvation
And the will to get along.
For every day is Christmas
When we chose to turn away
All prejudice and evil.
With love and peace we pray.

Christmas Day 2000

Beseech Me This

Beseech me this, my Lord I pray
That by your will, I might say
Let me do thy will thy way
My Lord, my Savior every day

The time goes by so swift these days
There's hardly time to kneel and pray
We watch our friendships pass away
With brotherhood, lost in the fray.
Our senses dulled, our thoughts are blurred
With hopes and dreams that ne'r occurred
Pressing on, not homeward bound
The rest we seek is never found.

You speak to us though grace and passion
The reply we give is but a ration.
Of what we own or what we treasure
Your love goes on without measure.
Today I seek to make it clear
A direction set, a mission clear
That you might guide my soul, I ask
That I might follow thy blessed task.

January 4, 2001

Faithfully They Gather

The snow on slate roofs slides
To the warmth of the morning sun
Shovels clear the sidewalks clear.
As the Sabbath day has begun
Faithfully they gather
In services near and far
On foot, by horse or wagon
By train, or boat or car.

Each day has its own beginning.
Each month and year does too.
With thoughtful prayer and service
He will gather there for you.

En route to Nassau Presbyterian

A Mother of Nature

Her sweetness is as soft as the first song of spring.
She welcomes the sun and the warmth found within.
A mask to this truth, she is always on guard.
Enjoying the treasures found in one's own backyard.
With trowel in hand she works out the weeds.
And with dreams inside she lays down her seeds.
Although the sun may dry, the rain moistens the soil.
The harvest she yields is worth all the toil.

A lady in waiting she is patient and kind.
Her strength and compassion is a wonderful find.
This mother of nature and all that she sows.
Changes seasons and surface wherever she goes.

March 7, 2001

For all that we know and seek to discover, is it no small wonder that what we understand the least is that which surrounds us each and every day? The universe is immense, and with each far-reaching search that we extend into deep space, we have yet to find any thing that even closely resembles our mother earth.

Miraculously she returns each day with new weather, seasons and surprises. Her surface is constantly changing, yet through God's will she yields not to the abuses and uncaring actions of man. With the winds she sends to carry seeds of renewal, we cast aside our trash on the roadsides that carry us. Hers will yield but a harvest of life, while the trash we sow yields but sorrow and illness.

I once wrote of the seeds in the core. When will learn of what we sow, so shall we reap.

The Light from Within

I am fairly confident that my wife and family must wonder sometime why I delve into so many new interests. Some are short lived, while others continue on and on. At times they interfere with my daily obligations, while other times they actually enhance my chores.

Regardless of whether it is reading verse from the bible, writing prose from the heart, volunteering work to our community or attending to a friend in trouble, lately I find myself going where my comfort level is strained by the risk of failure.

But as I grow older, I have begun to feel like one of those stones that, with time and increasing pressure, becomes hard and course on the surface.

That was, until my brother was dying. As painful as those days were, the special moments when I would see him focused my attention away from the less important, daily concerns. I came to see him, and myself, in a new light.

Although not apparent to me, at the time, I have come to see it as a reflection . . . of a light that was emerging from within. Out of the darkest moments of my life, God chipped away the crust of my hardening soul and exposed a beam of light from within. It had shown brightly on my brother's face when ever we'd meet; reflected off my wife's eyes when she'd comfort me in my lowest moments. Glowed happily when my son and I enjoy being together; and yes, cut through the mist of my tears as I read Matthew 9, Verse 1 on a special day in March.

The light from within is but one when first discovered. Like the prospector who catches a glimmer or sparkle in the rushing stream, his efforts are directed toward removing the debris and uncovering the layers that hide the treasure within.

A smooth round rock in a river's bed is beautiful when surrounded by others of differing textures, hues and shapes.

By comparison, a lump of coal can appear to lack charm or character. That is, until the coal is burned and it sends beams of light with warmth to those around it. That same piece of coal, if left buried beneath a mountain for thousands of years under extreme pressure will yield but one small diamond of brilliant possibilities.

But it takes a strong hand to unearth either piece of coal. It takes a wise hand to know how to generate the most light and warmth from the coal. And, it takes a gentle touch to expose the finest facets of a diamond to capture the light and reflect it upon those who happen to gaze upon it.

At times, are we not all but like lumps of coal . . . dark and mysterious, hiding within ourselves . . . unwilling or afraid to expose our inner most thoughts and weaknesses to others?

> There's a truth within that must begin
> With trust and self reflection
> A selfish doubt that will come out
> In times of confrontation
>
> The struggle of life begins with strife
> Upon leaving the warmth of the womb
> Once the process begins without conscious or sin
> It confronts us throughout our life.
>
> For wherever we turn, within us it burns
> The knowledge of who we are
> But with faith we can see,
> who we chose to be
> And journey toward a distant star

March 7, 2001

The Crescent Moon

The crescent moon above shines brightly through my window.
Although two thirds of it are clearly out of sight
In the morning mist I rise to watch its leaving
at the end of this long cold winter's night.

Today's spring morn will surely be a welcomed pleasure
To enjoy the warming of a bright and clear blue sky
With the snow and winter chill now far behind them.
Robins venture out and take wing to rise and fly

Like the moon's hidden side never seen in times of darkness
By the shadow of our earth's own shadow cast
Robins winter in the bushes and the by ways.
Hidden out of sight until snow and winter is past

For the best of life appears beyond what we are seeing
When listening closely to every sound and thought we've heard
The welcomed trust and understanding in His parables
With our faith in Christ we find the message in His Word.

March 20, 2001

The Spillway of Faith

Below our home at the end of North Spring Valley Road, a young child could experience the benefits of man's greatest efforts and nature's abundant bounty in peace and harmony. A large lake filled the valley from a man-made earthen dam. Here, where a stream once flowed through an Indian Reservation, arrowheads could now be uncovered whenever our neighbor's tilled their gardens for their spring planting.

Like the Indian children that once ran along the valley's ridge, my brothers and I enjoyed exploring the forests that surrounded the coves of the lake. Marching up to the dam's spillway on the far side of the lake, the dark forest was a sharp contrast to the wide span of the lake and the long flat top of the dam.

The steep earthen dam now towered above the pines, and although topped off with rock and soil, even the mighty dam served Mother Nature's purposes. Nearby woodchucks would venture out onto its steep grassy slopes in the spring, and delicate small buttercups and wild violets blanketed it in summer. Crawfish would dart along the rock-filled banks as mallard ducks often swam above.

This was a place of harmony between man and nature . . . both past and present.

As young students, one of the best places to study could be found at the base of the dam's spillway. Here ebbing sheets of fresh water rushed down the wide concrete structure in these cascading waves. In the early spring thaw, the lake would rise to its highest point. The excitement of the thundering waves at the base of the spillway enveloped the larger rocks in the stream below, making a crossing all but impossible.

Later in the spring, when the water's pace had slowed, my brothers, neighbors and I would enjoy spreading out Later in the Later in the spring, when the water's pace had slowed, my brothers, neighbors and I would enjoy spreading out to our own individual rocks or fallen logs to read, write or prepare our homework in peaceful respite. The spillway's steady beat was a welcomed backdrop to the babbling of the brook, which wound itself through the forest and farms below us. In the summer we would skip flat stones across the lake's calmer surface, or take off our shoes and socks to surf barefoot down the algae-covered spillway into the cool water below.

Today I reflect on these memories with a different perspective. Eager to find a similar place of refuge from the challenges of adult life, I reflect upon our Lord's creation and places like these where nature and man could coexist in harmony. Like the water behind a man-made dam, faith can well up inside us until we can no longer contain it, and our love flows in the spillway of faith.

> The spillway of faith can be found in one's heart
> When it swells up inside us and we're willing to part
> With the wealth of experience and compassionate pride
> Of the love of our Savior we can no longer hide.

> Life's lessons best learned by the grace of this land
> A warm welcome of love, by the touch of His hand.
> To cascade forth in waves, between heaven and earth
> He speaks to us softly, and preserves what we're worth.

> More precious than silver, more cherished than gold
> The love that He sends us, cannot be bought, nor ever be sold.

> For life is a journey, one can never regret
> The faces and place, and the people we've met.
> When sharing with others *may your* feelings run deep
> So forever within *you,* your memories will keep

Flowing over the spillway, on to far, distant shores
Returning in spring time to bring stories and lores.
The love that flows freely when abundance is clear
Will return to *you* safely, so honest and dear.

March 30, 2001

The Chill Before Dawn

The chill, in the last few moments just before dawn, feels to be the coldest of most every night. It seems that the burdens that we shed from the day before are being replaced by the challenges that we know will face us in the days ahead.

Like the pack mule who has labored under the weight of cargo carried on its back, when once removed, there are but a few moments when its weary back is relaxed and exposed to the cool night air. A chill is felt . . . and the burro shivers when his damp coat of hair is exposed.

We are not unlike this beast of burden. For we too carry many weights and responsibilities throughout our lives. On some days the load is light and the journey seems somewhat shorter. On other days, it seems that the burdens placed upon us feel to be greater than the strength within us. Those are the journeys that seem to never end. But they do. They all eventually do.

Like the mule whose daily routine must sometimes feel like a life of boring, repetitive and futile existence, our spirits are sometimes broken. We keep our heads down looking only at the path beneath our feet, and march in a direction determined by others. Indeed, we can often become so numb to the effort that we begin to loose interest in what burdens we actually carry, where we are headed and the mission of our work.

In corporate America mission building is a task taken seriously by any forward thinking organization. Here in the church, retreats are conducted to remove us from our daily burdens and focus our attention to a higher calling. Away from the distractions of routine schedules, mundane labors and root studies, families must take vacations to re-establish their sense of commitment; a commitment to each other, and the importance of their love.

Yes, a chill still runs down my spine in the early moments before dawn. This is the time that I take to reflect, and shed the burdens of yesterday's work. After I awake my son for school, and before I set up the iron for another shirt to be pressed. I pray to our Lord. Thanking him for the end of another successful journey; reflecting on the steps taken, unburdening myself of mistakes that I have made and preparing for the mission that now awaits me.

Thousands of years ago a small donkey carried a weight so great that it changed the world forever. No, his cargo wasn't heavy, and although his journey was long, something was different. The sky was brighter, the caravan was much smaller, and unbeknownst to him, the mission was clearer; for although a manger of fresh straw and hay awaited him, on this journey, he would enjoy sharing his burden with the world. Giving up his home for another, for when placed before him in a manager, the burden was so small; so frail that he wondered how he ever thought it to be a burden at all.

This is what Christ does. Although at times following the mission in our lives seems to be a burden, remember that small donkey of long ago. When caught up in the spirit of Christ you know that something is different. The sky is definitely brighter, the caravan, although somewhat longer, is filled with people whom you enjoy working. And yes, the burden will be lighter.

Know that a wonderful event awaits us, and our labors. And the chill of morning will be followed by the warmth of His Son.

> In early morning dawn, before children rise and yawn
> There's a new day filled with mystery and wonder.
>
> For although the day is long, in Christ's faith you will be strong.
> And the burdens that you bear He'll put asunder.

April 3, 2001

In the Eyes of a Child

In the eyes of a child there is wonder and good
Seeing only the beauty of life that one could
Before wisdom is gained by the trials that we seek
A child builds on the merits that come from the meek.

A world full of wonder he finds in each day,
Regardless of problems that might come his way
In the eyes of a child there's no room for dark skies
And his ears will not welcome false statements or lies.

Her voice will not waiver or falter with doubt
When expressing her feeling there's no need to shout
An innocent flower that welcomes the sun
The shadow she casts is a sweet loving one.

April 13, 2001

Before the Bud Opens

Before the bud opens in the soft morning light
Its heart will it shelter from the cold evening night
Arising to greet us with the first morning dew
His majesty's grace blossoms out to reach you.

The daffodils' petals announce another spring season
The azaleas that follow give us cause and good reason
To welcome His bounty and His Son's saving grace
To a world of His making, what a wonderful place.

When the petals have fallen and the warm summer sun
Settles high in the sky and brings warmth to each one
And the plantings take root and continue to grow
We must take stock in our faith and let the world know

For a season will come when we walk hand-in-hand
And peace will return o'er the oceans and land
When the buds that protect us and our hearts within
Will open up brightly and relinquish our sin.

April 28, 2001

Out of the Mist of Histories Past

Out of the mist of histories past
Their names are etched in monuments cast
For history is learned on the face of a stone
Their legacy told in the lives we have known

Memories gained in discoveries now found
Of stories learned from this now hallowed ground
These are the souls that pioneered to this place
Who now we do welcome by His holy grace.

To these brave men, women and children we pray
Who pressed on before us to show us the way
That throughout time let your heart lead your way
To a home you'll discover in this town, on this day.

Let us honor their journey.

Princessville Cemetery
Lawrenceville, New Jersey
May 4, 2001

The Indigo Bunting

There is a small, deep blue bird that can barely be seen. He hides in the darkest retreats of the woods, or high in the canopy of the tallest trees, sheltered from the light above and from view from below.

Once he chooses his home, he is as reliable as the promise of each new day. In the early morning, his shrill three tunes rise before the break of dawn. Although he is gone for the better part of the day, when the evening dusk settles in, he and his tune will return.

On a few occasions we have spotted this beautiful bird. Although seldom seen, his brilliant, deep indigo body is stunning when exposed to the light of day. This is what he is known for, and how he has come to be known as the Indigo Bunting.

This morning as I lay in bed, his tune returned to my back yard. As evasive as he is from my sight, the first notes of his tune brought back a strong memory; a memory hidden deep in my past, a memory of my father's whistle. When was enjoying the completion of a successful chore at our old farmhouse, or when he wanted one of his pure bred boxers to come in for dinner, he would whistle the first of these three notes.

Perhaps he heard this song when he used to rise before daybreak to begin a long commute to work. Or maybe it was when he returned just in time for supper at the end of a long day. But for my family and me, it has come to be a sound of reassurance.

Over the years this sound has become a source of comfort for my brothers and me, knowing that our father was home, and had returned from a long day or week at work. Out of sight, but never out of mind.

I believe that a father's role in the family is one that requires a strong faith. Although seldom physically present, he must forge an air of responsibility and stability.

And then there is the especially strong faith of the wife. As a mother, she bears the challenging task of maintaining a home for her children while balancing the responsibilities of a wife.

Both parents are aware of their roles and responsibilities. Given the importance of these challenges, they rise each morning to face a new day. Like the Indigo Bunting the beauty of their efforts is seldom seen or recognized but their faithful presence continues on in the lives that they touch, and the children they raise.

May 7, 2001

Where no wood is,
there the fire goes out

Where the heart sings, the voice will learn to shout
Where the soul finds peace, you will find our Lord to be there caring
Where time is not, there will be ample time for sharing.

Who rises with the wind, will discover worlds of wonder.
Who shelters from the storm, puts adventure far asunder.
Who reasons without prayer, consults but with a fool.
Who with his word offends, will never get to rule.

What light beneath a basket, guides not a journey bound
What hand that is not extended, will ne'er a friend be found.
What words will not be spoken, no healing can begin.
What wisdom never chosen, a choice that leads to sin.

When but one life can be saved, there's no fear found in the grave.
When in the sacrifice of One, God's only gracious son.
When the world is not at peace, is when we learn to reach.
When His blessings find their way, your heart will learn to pray.

May 17, 2001

Disciples

Have you ever watched a good movie or read a book that was so great that you wish it wouldn't end? Or, perhaps you enjoyed imagining how it might have continued. These very thoughts come to mind when I recall the journeys of Our Savior and his Disciples that He chose to lead.

When Jesus walked among us he sought out those in need. Regardless of how others may judge his actions, he judged not others, but ventured where others dared not go. Among the Lepers and the infirmed, the outcasts and the accused, his faith in salvation was unshaken and his purpose unquestioned.

So were the journeys of his Disciples, who after his crucifixion and resurrection, spread out to see that this great story continue.

Does the movie end there? Was the story so well written, and so clearly told that we are satisfied to watch the credits and return to our daily lives? Or do we imagine how it might continue if we were a Disciple of Christ.

"Commit random acts of kindness" is a bumper sticker that I always enjoy seeing. If this simple suggestion were followed by everyone, how much different would we be than the Disciples or followers of Jesus?

There was a new movie out recently, which I still intend to see. The title is "Pay it Forward" and I understand that its premise is very similar to the bumper sticker phrase and the mission of Jesus' Disciples.

For you see, thousands of years ago, our sins were paid forward. With the blood of Christ, our hands have been washed clean. Cleaned of the dirt under our nails that lingered like bad memories of the mistakes we have made. Cured of the blisters we bore from hard work toward selfish pursuits. Through Jesus Christ, our hands are caressed in spite of the comfort we failed to extend to others.

In this world, and more particularly in this country, we are undaunted in our pursuit of our freedom of choice. The freedom to change one's mind and set a new course can be a blessing or a curse, depending on the choices we make.

Based on our own experiences, the wisdom we impart to others is not unlike that which the Disciples chose to share from their time with Jesus. Their role in our salvation continues on today through the fascinating books of the bible. Psalms sing praise to creation and God's holy works. Parables express in but a few words the deeper meaning of Christ's lessons. And John and Mathew share with us the exact words of Christ in a manner that draws us closer to imagining the very presence of Christ.

Like Job we chose to curse and complain of the burdens we bear and the injustice that has befallen us.

Not unlike Thomas we question the validity of that which we hear. Until we can touch the very wounds where our Savior was nailed to the cross, we chose to question and doubt.

But when Jesus touches you, be it in an hour of great sorrow, or a moment of welcomed relief ... look around you. Fear not to reach out, whether you are suffering or if you are in a position to comfort. Administer to workings of our Lord, so that the long list of credits may continue. As Disciples in Christ, you have been chosen to see that this movie may never end.

June 7, 2001

Hosanna

Some time ago I wrote of the chill before dawn, and of how a small donkey's burdens can begin the journey of a life so great. The life of our Savior began on the back of a donkey. And before He died he once again rode on a small donkey as we hailed Hosanna. Our Savior, our King, triumphantly welcomed by children with palm branches laid before Him. He whose birth was heralded by angels is he whose arrival was sought by wise men, is he whose life would not be tempted by Satan for all the power on earth.

He who returned to us knowing the fate that awaited Him.

How would we fare if we knew what fate awaits us? If you knew that today's important presentation was doomed for failure? Or if in the morning paper we could read of events that would befall our neighbors. What if you knew the right stock to pick, one that would make you countless riches because you knew of a major catastrophe that would hurt millions of others, but would place you at the top. Would you be the same person that you are today? Or would your life be somewhat different. Wouldn't it be changed forever, regardless of which action you did or didn't take?

It would be an awesome responsibility; a burden beyond belief.

Every day we make decisions. Some will affect us at that very moment. Others will almost seem to lie in wait; until a day when the results of a decision made today springs up before us in the future. Sometimes they shock us and we wonder how this could have happened. Other times we are pleasantly surprised. And then, we recall . . . a time from the past when a burden had to be borne, and a decision had to be made.

Today is that day, my friends. Today's decisions are those that must be made. In the faith and understanding, that the burden we bear is a small burden compared to the wonderful arrival that awaits us in His glory. The palms our Savior will rest beneath our tired and weary feet. The journey's end will be glorious beyond all wonder and imagination.

Believe. Believe in the Father; in the Son. And the Holy Spirit will be found within you.

May 20, 2001

Of All the Senses

Of all the senses that we possess, the greatest one is faith. For each of our senses alone are wonderful, but what brings them together for the good of mankind is faith.

The sweet songs in the morning mist, suggests that unseen birds have risen. The warmth on my back as I sit and read, is a likely sign that the sun is up, or is it? Although the chill is lessening, and the words in my bible are now easier to read, I do not know if the sun behind me has yet crossed the horizon, or is merely inching its way closer.

The sweet smell of flowers that awaken my senses . . . do they come from our flowers, or the flowers in my neighbor's back yard, or are they carried from far beyond on the air that now stirs the hair on my arms?

What we see, hear, smell and feel tells us so much. Life can be described in so many ways, but without reference to our senses, it is almost impossible to comprehend.

That is where faith steps in: to bring it all together. The creator of all that we sense, with the miracle of life at His very hand, is a blessing. Remove but one, and faith will fill the void. The other senses will heighten and life will continue.

It is easy to believe what our senses tell us. They can be a blessing when enjoying the pleasures in life, and seem to be a curse in times of pain, sorrow or fear.

A small baby's cry can seem able to pierce through lead walls. Their gentle skin can develop an intensely painful rash, which is confirmed by the pain reflected in their eyes and the frown on their face. Of course we can't forget that unique aroma. The first indication of where the source of our child's trouble may be found.

But when we attend to the problems that our senses have directed us, a miracle occurs. This will become the same child whose coo is now music to our ears. Whose skin is as soft a silk, and whose eyes are as bright as the morning stars. Once properly bathed and powdered, this same small child is a joy to hold in one's arms. Their infectious smile cannot be left unreturned by all who gaze in awe and wonder.

Yes, this is the blessing of the faithful. Those who trust their senses, and those who attend to the world's pain, suffering and sorrows.

Our senses always serve a purpose. Be it to engage or to repel, to encourage or discourage, to refute or to welcome.

As I grow older, I've come to notice that my senses are diminishing in strength and clarity. My eyes are drier and my lenses need to be adjusted more frequently. My food requires more seasoning, as my sense of smell is less acute. More and more frequently I must ask for words to be repeated.

We live in a society where we want to deny and avoid the aging process. But here again faith steps in.

Although my sight may be failing, my vision of who I want to be is finally coming into focus. Despite the fact that my hearing may be lessening, it seems as though my understanding is expanding. As my hands become numb for lack of circulation, with every person I meet, my feelings of compassion and empathy for others is increased. Though food may be lacking flavor, my hunger for the word of God and His holy grace sustains me throughout the day. Recounting the abundance of our Savior's love and compassion has found its way into my vocabulary.

These changes confirm a new sense that renews our youth, as we grow older. The renewing sense of faith is what brings us together before it is time to depart.

>The rain upon my weathered brow
>Feels fresh and cool upon me
>Though my vision fails, my heart prevails
>A new sense of faith, I come to see.

Selah

May 25, 2001

Out of the Woods

Out of the woods to the new light of day,
We seek our Lord's guidance in the words that we pray.
Like Job who was beaten and battered unto dust
We seek out the answers and wisdom from those that we trust

Blind to the perils and trials that others must face
Of our own shame and sorrows is what brings us disgrace

For though "man unto man" is where we place our concern
Through "the Son unto Father" that together we learn

That the world is His creation and we are but one
Of the miracles residing beneath the warm sun

We make our lives better by not disturbing this land
But by reaching out toward Him and extending our hand

In thoughtful praise and thanksgiving this day we do pray
That His blessings and wisdom will through Christ come our way.

June 6, 2001

How Gracious Is He

How gracious is He that grants us our wishes
Be they wise or of little time thought
To welcome our choices by one who rejoices
His love and respect be they sought.

We bitterly challenge the words that we read
And His efforts that clear out the way.
Then question why we fail, though His compassion will prevail
As forgiveness for us do we pray.

The journey of man can be a great blessing
For each morning can begin a new life
But mistakes of the past though they seldom will last
Can bring eternal damnation and strife.

This morning I pray as a life pasts away
From an action of foolish self pride
To put innocent lives in harms way, on a now fateful day
In God's hands may your fate now reside.

May we seek His compassion in how we respond
And become not the evil that's done
Let this day end but fast, and may our memories last
Of the Father, our Savior, the Son.

June 11, 2001

Oh Lord

Oh Lord, Creator of all that we see and the knowledge that we seek. Open our eyes, as the soft morning light, to the truth that awaits us. Moisten our lips like the dew on the petals of a rose, that we may open our voices in heartfelt prayers and supplications. May you make our hearts warm to the compassion of others, while strengthening our resolve when cast before those among us who seek our harm. Let not our heads turn from the face of truth, at the sight of those in need, for such is the image of our own fate.

At thy will, so shall we wane. With thy blessings, so shall we prosper. From thy hand so shall we be judged. By thy mercy may we be forgiven.

Selah

June 13, 2001

Priorities

- Faith in the Lord
- Love of Family
- Friendship of Man
- Strength of Conviction
- Value of Truth
- Pursuit of Wisdom
- Power of Love
- Dreams to Follow
- Memories to Cherish
- Time to Enjoy
- Tears for Sorrow
- Happiness to Share
- Wealth to Give
- Knowledge to Gain
- Compassion to Spread
- Mistakes to Admit
- Pride to Relinquish

To Brave Hearts, Strong Wills & Kind Souls
May They Be All In One, And "One" In All Of Us.

June 16, 2001

The Evening's Calm

The evening's calm is but brief solace to the weary. Anxious for the well-deserved rest that awaits them, they gather around to reflect on the day's events.

The city street bustles outside, as an arm rises out to reach the shelter's gray, wool blanket. Memories are the only possessions that one dares to carry. Kept about one, for a warmth from the cold found about and the emptiness found within.

As they lie in winter on steel grates and manhole covers, the shadows that we cast in passing cannot compete with the cold indifference that we share with those less fortunate. Harder than the strong, round steel beneath them, we shield ourselves from the truth of the spoken and written word:

"The rich and the poor are alike in that our Lord made them all. Proverbs 22:2

As God does not judge us by our possessions, who are we to judge others by their lack thereof? If one is without faith, does the Lord turn his back, I dare not say. For one need only look to the sacrifice of His only Son, to understand the full extent to which His love will go.

As full as our lives may seem by the possessions that surround us, we are no different than the homeless who seek warmth and shelter. We too need to lift up our arm and praise our Father for the memories of our Savior. For they too will protect us from the cold found about and the emptiness found within.

June 18, 2001

Through Cresting Waves

How crisp and clear the morning breeze
On songs of birds, out in the trees.
As spirits rise, the clouds give way
The storm is past; it's time to pray.

In tempest winds our faith prevailed
Through cresting waves onward we sailed.
In darkest nights, no stars to see
On waters walked, He called to me.

"Be not afraid" in faith you'll see
The strength and courage found in me.
Our Father's love will never falter
Believe in Christ, beyond the altar.

June 24, 2001

Compassion

In time all of mankind will come to know Him; for He resides within us all. With each new discovery of one's self and one's purpose in life, we all come one step closer to a universal understanding.

His glory is within and shines every time we reach out to those in need. This is the glory of conquest, the conquest of self-righteousness by caring for others as He cares for us.

Compassion is a direction to be chosen. If broken down, it is the "compass" to where "I" move "on." When one feels broken down, it is what we seek in others. Compassion is what our savior, Jesus felt for those he met. It is what others sought in following His word. Like the needle in a compass, all who sought His loving kindness looked toward Him. His is our magnetic North. Regardless of which direction we chose, His is the one constant in our life; the assurance of the way to all who seek Him.

> *No matter what the course that's chosen*
> *Or wherever, I may be bound.*
> *His compassion sets my faith before me*
> *A true direction will be found.*

June 26, 2001

One Life is But the Cost

What strength is there when fear runs near
And hope is all but lost
To give in prayer a freedom found
Our life is but the cost

To venture out in search of peace
His guidance that we seek.
A blessed heart, His welcomed gift
An inheritance for the meek.

For our souls are one before we come
To our final resting place
In His blessed hands, He doth command
By His wisdom and His grace.

This day is mine for when I find
My salvation through His word
Tomorrow will be a new day for me
Through the greatness of my Lord.

June 28, 2001

The Blessings of Diversity

The blessings of variety
For everywhere I see
A world of peace and harmony
Found in diversity

Few greater gifts He gives to us
Than to recognize our place
Is not one of greater dominance
By the color of our face.

The world is one great mystery
Full of miracles and wonder
Though we seek to find its answers
By the truths we put asunder.

The truth is right before us
If in each day that we begin
To question not our diversity
But seek the love that's found within

For each life is irreplaceable
And every song that must be heard
Is unique within the harmony
Found in the message of His word.

For the bible speak in volumes
Of what our lives should be
To welcome the world's diversity
That is found in what we see.

July 6, 2001

Closer Than One Knows

We look outward for salvation
Into the stars up high
With prayers unto the heavens
Looking upward toward the sky

Our songs are sung in harmony
With praises long and loud
But salvation is not found up there
Amongst the passing cloud.

The spirit of our Savior
Is much closer than one knows
With heartfelt prayer and kindness
Everywhere His spirit grows.

In the song of life discover
Who you were meant to be
Salvation you'll discover
Is the song of you and He.

July 7, 2001

When All That One Has

When all that one has
Can be found in one's faith
Like the Apostle Paul
When he came to the gate

At heaven's doors
He had abandoned his past
Unto our Savior he followed
With a faith meant to last.

In life we seek happiness
And collect all we desire
At the gate we'll face judgment
Be it heaven or fire.

Like Paul we will enter
As we came to this place
With little to bear
But the smile on our face

And like those all around
Who welcomed us here
When we leave let our faith
Conquer all that we fear.

July 8, 2001

Dear Lord

You welcome us into your open arms with gracious love and warm compassion. We come to you with our head bowed low and our once proud spirit crushed into the dust; for we have seen our reflection and it is sorely wanting.

With the kindness shown to us through your son, our Savior, your hand reaches out to touch our face and we are anew. Rising from the grave of our own making, your faith lifts us out of the pit. Our spirit is filled with the eternal light of peace and our fears and pain fall back to earth like the rain.

To replenish, renew and bring life back into our hearts, shower your love upon us. Through Christ may we find shelter and the strength to carry on. In this we do pray. Amen

July 13, 2001

Reflections

What is a reflection? In a mirror, it is that which others see. To a wise man it is remembering a thought, time or comment with an inquisitive mind. For those seeking salvation, it is an earnest confession of sin and a heartfelt repentance.

Therefore one could say that reflections can be seen in mirrors, water, memories and yes, the written word.

Although many written words exist, man has not always known the written word. Cave dwellers and hunters and gathers sought a means to express themselves through images and stories portrayed on cave wall paintings or carved in stones.

Later on, script and hieroglyphics were developed and paper scrolls captured records and historic events.

Today we read volumes of words through newspapers, books, television, and computers.

But I ask you, as the deluge of written words assaults us every day, how much of it do we retain? Daily newspapers speak of events around the corner and around the globe. Yet we discard them in green cans to be "recycled" again.

How much of it encourages us to reflect on the stories within? If well written the written word will encourage us to reflect and take action. Much of today's written words are meant to entertain, escape or amuse. Like the newspapers, books, televisions or monitors that we view, many of these words are discarded, resold, saved (though seldom reviewed) or maybe recycled.

There are times, however, when the written word speaks to us at a very special moment. In times when the soul has sunken so low, or excitement and happiness cannot be contained, that spoken or written word comes to life.

There is one written word however. One that recounts and reflects upon the actions of all mankind and nature is the same One that speaks to us in volumes and has stood the test of time. These words give cause for reflection. These words guide us in our daily lives and have changed the course of nations.

Historians, scholars and seminarians have explored the bible's written words for decades. Few books have been the cause of debates and differences of opinion. Crusades of faith swept over continents in vicious battles of yesterday, and today crusades continue over the airwaves and Internet with words intended to divide our nation.

Now is the time to reflect. Not on how right or strongly one feels about issues of the day . . . but how one's words can hurt others without forgiveness.

I once wrote of how forgiveness can be found in a vase full of crystal intentions. In a reflection of one's self seek thee forgiveness in yourself, of all you meet and most important of all, from the Lord.

July 14, 2001

His is the Light

His is the light that retreats not unto fear
His is the word that we long to hear.
For that which is missing, not found in the heart
The faith that we cherish, from here we must start.

A child unto Christ we are all but one
The wisdom we seek must come from His Son
Jesus, our Savior, our way to toward the light
The path that He leadeth is honest and right.

July 15, 2001

All in Good Time

All in good time is what they say
All in good time what come what may
All in good time this day I pray
All in good time but every day.

To wait on the Lord is a special task
To wait on the Lord in all that we ask
To wait on the Lord and be patient and clear
To wait on the Lord with the prayers that he'll hear

His majesty is good and right
His majesty will win the fight
His majesty He will find in me
His majesty will set us free

For unto us He gave His Son
For unto us His Will be done
For unto us what come what may
For unto us this day I pray

July 16, 2001

How Plentiful The Harvest

How plentiful the harvest
When men cannot be found.
To spread the word of Jesus
When pain and woes abound.

He came to save the sinners
From Satan's mighty grasp
The need of every shepherd
A lifelong daunting task.

Though sorrow may afflict you
And happiness is naught
Consider Jesus' mission
When facing what He sought

The multitude of suffering
For everywhere He went
They came to him in search of
The faith and love God sent

For we are all but shepherds
Once awakened to His grace
To help the needs of others
There can be no hiding place.

July 18, 2001
Matthew 9:36-38

Loving Kindness and Tender Mercies

Loving kindness and tender mercies
Is what He shares with us.
Everlasting to everlasting
Until we turn to dust

From this day forth the path you'll take
When reaching for His hand
A steady walk, a tender talk
The strength to take a stand.

Consult with He that guards thy soul
And hearken to His word
In time you'll see what comes to thee
Is like a mighty sword.

In thy hand the sword can be
A source of great destruction
Sharp and bright to reflect the light
Of thy inner soul's salvation.

To guard one's faith in a world of hate
With loving kindness in your heart
Be so ever clear and with faith so near
Tender mercies you'll impart.

July 23, 2001
Psalm 103

What Does He See

What does He see when He looks at me
Amongst all in the world He commands
From the mountains on high, just below His great sky
To each grain, that He knows in the sands.

What will you do when He reaches for you
Will you reach out in prayer, or be torn?
Rejoice with your heart, from that day will you start
And a new life in Christ will be born.

For wherever we go, we really don't know
What is planned to occur on that day
With our fate in His hand, matters not where we stand
For the journey of Christ is the way.

July 25, 2001

The Bench in My Garden

The bench in my garden
Has its back toward the sun
The shade from its trees
Can protect everyone

There are stones at it posts
And with bark on the ground
In the early spring morning
There is nary a sound

With my bible in hand
I walk out to this place
As the birds and squirrels
Bring a smile to my face

Their songs and their antics
Wake my ears and tired eyes
As the sun slowly rises
To a brilliant sunrise

With each verse that I read
My thoughts now awake
To the wisdom and warnings
That our actions forsake

Through the blessings of Psalms
And the prayers that I read
Answer all of my questions
And fulfill all my needs

Though the garden will beckon
And the bench will provide
A comfort and respite
Not a place will I hide

For with praise to our Lord
By His blessings and care
Through these poems and my prayers
From my bench, will I share.

The bench in my garden
Is wide and has room
If you join me each morning
We can cast out the gloom.

July 28, 2001

The Dog Days of Summer

They call these the "dog days of summer"; a time in late July when we slow down into a relaxed mode. Work gives way to hours spent reflecting on the more important aspects of life. An evening stroll, a few more minutes in bed before rising, an observance of nature, be it a wasp with a worm, a praying mantis with a wasp or a butterfly in flight.

Time seems to slow down in these days. Children set out lemonade stands, and the attendance at church is somewhat smaller and more casual.

Later in the day, a backyard barbeque simmers the fresh fish of the seas, as sweet white corn from the earth boils in water on the stove inside. The elderly sit outside their homes and the lawns give way to bouts of bocce and badminton. The clanking sound of horseshoes in the woods, as a father and son enjoy a few special moments together. In the evening, a movie is watched with friends and family. It relaxes our thoughts before retiring to the comfort of sleep.

Reports of an approaching rain are a blessed break to the heat, as the last remnants of the spring floras give way to rising hues of brown and tan.

Autumn will soon be upon us, as the fireflies dwindle in number and the mosquitoes seek their last evening meals.

The night skies seem to beckon us, as constellations seem closer and passing clouds almost glow. The occasional site of a falling star sweeps by in pursuit of our wonder and childhood imagination.

Such are these days of summer. When the peaceful respite of life is without worry, and presence of a loved one at your side, or in your memory, brings a special comfort to the heart.

This is when I pray that the grace, harmony and blessings of our Lord's creations shared in these special moments with you will bring us all closer together. With praise and song remember the simple pleasures that He has set before us, at His table, and rejoice. Rejoice in the comfort of His home ... where all are welcomed.

July 29, 2001

By Bread Alone

Man does not live by bread alone
His soul will hunger, he must atone
To the will of God and the love of Christ
Once accepting His faith, he lives but twice

Once in a world that is sought by man
Again in heaven by the grace of His hand
We seek earthly treasures to feed our yearning
In heaven the pleasures we'll forever be learning

For once we acknowledge His love and compassion
Our hunger He'll fill with more than our ration
To share with others who struggle each day
May the blessings we share fulfill hunger we pray

July 31, 2001

The Master Builder

The master builder restores our lives
Through His works and kind salvation
In moments of despair you will find Him there
At the head of every God fearing nation.

To lead without faith is like a builder without level
Never knowing how straight the stone cast.
By the time that one's through, not a house will he rule
And the structure he built will not last.

August 3, 2001

Grace & Understanding

What is grace and understanding?

When seeking guidance from our Lord and Savior, can the mist be lifted from our eyes? Beneath the veil of the bride is the face of love. The reflections of our own innermost desires are lifted as the veil of understanding is raised and our one true passion is revealed. Such is one's relation with God.

The bible makes many references to the bridegroom and in these words I have come to understand the message of salvation. When one is prepared to commit their very existence to serve the Lord, a bond is made; a bond that cannot be challenged, nor broken, not now or forever.

Grace and understanding ... one cannot exist, but for the presence of the other. This I have come to know as a blessing of our Lord.

August 5, 2001

after reading ...
"You Have Captured God's Heart"
August 4
Grace for The Moment by Max Lucado

The Twilight

The twilight sounds a time to rest
When views and vision cannot be best
The shadows gray and dark of night
Removes most of the images from our sight.

The day is gone; we've done our best
We've met the charge and passed the test
Tonight the deer will rise with fawn
Tomorrow's day, we'll begin at dawn.

We'll rise with clouds rubbed from our eyes
To a bible's verse of truth, not lies.
Our Lord will clear the mist of night
Until day's events, returns twilight.

Twilight is so very different from the dawn to me. Have you ever spent a day without using an electric light or fire to extend or start the day? To remove oneself from any source of artificial light seems almost impossible for one who lives in the northeastern U.S.

I recall special times when observing the lights of nature is a wonder all its own. A night in upstate New York, when the northern lights waved across the skies in a spectacular array; then there are the shooting stars that catch us off guard on an evening stroll or a long journey's night. The stars I'll never forget . . . from a Texas panhandle trip with my brother, the West Virginia skies with my cousin, or from a walk on the beach with my wife and son. Each was a special time of peace and harmony with one of God's greatest creations, light.

We share it. We seek it. We are a part of it in how we live our lives.

"The light of day" is a phrase often used to express the exposure of truth. For man, "one must see it to believe it." But there is another light. It cannot be seen to the naked eye, but is known throughout the world. We rely on it often. When we rise to greet a new day, or prepare to retire in the evening, it is there. It is the light of the faithful.

In twilight's dim outlines and gray images, it is what guides us around obstacles. During moments of difficult decisions, be they
child rearing, test taking, goal seeking, career making or life threatening, that is when this light appears inside us. And that is when it is seen by others around us. You'll see it in the homes, schools, offices and factories. In the fields and farms, hospices and hospitals; churches, synagogues, temples and places of worship . . . All bear this light.

The Twilights of Mankind

Believe it or not, twilight of man has occurred many times: the dark ages, the crusades, the great depression, the world wars, and most recently, the Y2K rollover.

Can you imagine for just one moment, what it would have been like had the fears and worries of a worldwide blackout actually occurred during the Y2K rollover? Darkness may have set in and as sure as every day would be met with chaos and mayhem . . . the greatest light of all would prevail.

The light of creation, the light of wisdom and the light of understanding; everyone would reach for it, in his or her moment of concern or despair. For the light of faith, it will always be there, for our Lord has assured it. For every twilight will be followed by a new dawn. And through His Son, our Savior . . . so shall the darkness of death be overcome by the light of faith.

August 9, 2001

Wisdom and Understanding

What stands in the way of wisdom? Where is understanding born? We seek knowledge as a lost soul reaches for a compass, not knowing where he is, nor which direction lies salvation. With each step taken in any direction the odds are greatly skewed that they are headed in the wrong direction.

> Wither Thou leadest, I will go.
> Whatever Thou teachest, we will know.
> Whenever Thou callest, all will show.
> Wherever Thou touchest, life shall grow.

When one surrenders one's self to the Lord, understanding is born. Whoever steps aside, and let's faith lead on, finds wisdom right before them.

August 16, 2001

Children's Children

Children's children are the crown of old men;
and the glory of children are their fathers.

Proverbs 17:6

We are children's children. Our fathers are Jacob and Aaron, Moses and David, Matthew, Peter and the disciples of our Lord and Savior. They are our glory for they have dealt with us fairly and loved us for their time and for generations yet to be born.

Peace and harmony in the sight of God were their dreams for us. Driven by an unquenchable thirst for the blessings that flow from the Lord, they became a wellspring of hope and prosperity for all who followed.

As the waves that thunder upon the beach, undaunted they pounded their message home. Like gale force winds and lightning strikes against an ocean deep, they too were challenged and persecuted by nay Sayers, kings' armies and the throngs of disbelievers. But onward they pressed to distant shores. As the waves so change the coastal shores, so did they change the faith of men.

And as their children's children, so can we.

To the glory of the Father, the Son and the Holy Spirit, Amen

August 21, 2001

With One Option Left

With no option is left in the eye of the storm
Where no direction is safe and there's no place to get warm
Stop wherever you stand and look up to the sky
With prayers to the Lord and prepared to die

This is the time when you'll put far behind
Those meaningless notions that have cluttered your mind
Like strength in position, or immeasurable pride
Were but fleeting fancies leaving no place to hide.

Ripped from one's moorings like a ship in a gale
You'll toss and you'll turn and forget how to sail
Until the message hits home and you fear not your fate
By the grace of His hand He will open the gate

With wisdom and knowledge He will open your eyes
You'll relinquish all fears and reach up towards the skies
Salvation is a blessing that can weather the past
The redemption that follows is a blessing that lasts.

There's but one option present to the strong, faithful few
To the tired and the weary, by the One we all knew
His salvation is found in the cross that we see
Forgiveness and blessings between you and between me.

August 26, 2001

After reading "Rescued by Heaven" in the eye of the storm . . . **GRACE FOR THE MOMEN**T by Max Lucado

On a Mission of Truth

Witness with me the works of our Lord
And be not silent nor fear
The truth that is told will not waiver, nor scold
For your heart will be all that they hear.

In a world of deceit when many you'll meet
Have agendas that cannot be known
Raise you hands and but pray, for there will come a day
As a witness, the truth will be shown.

Gather together thy thoughts and prepare to be taught
Of the power through faith in His Son
When you open your heart as a witness you'll start
On a mission of truth, you'll have won.

August 30, 2001

At the Foot of His Throne

For that which is tattered, be it our turn to mend
With words full of wisdom, in praise we must send
A message to others of His saving grace
Our Lord and our Savior we know we must face.

At the foot of His throne, we all must atone
And rise up from the dark, and leave empty the grave
Whence compassion is shared, knowing no one is spared
Through His faith and forgiveness that we might be saved.

August 31, 2001

The Garden of Peace

In this garden of peace may the memories grow
Of who we are and of what we now know
For the heart of true wisdom is surrounded by light
The future begins here, what a wondrous sight.

The sides of this garden are enclosed all by life
May it serve as a respite from work and from strife
At the center you're senses see all that you need
That which cannot be bought through excess or through greed.

With recreation and food may your body find health
Through the wisdom of others may you discover true wealth
Keep the arts and the music, always close at your side
With the beauty of nature, may you always reside

In this garden of nature find the beauty within
For yours is the future and through life you will win
May you welcome all others who come into this space
With the beauty of peace that you find in this place.

September 1, 2001

But One Freedom

Man speaks of freedom as if man has any say in it at all. Freedom comes not from a grant given by others, but by surrendering oneself to the Lord. From whence all power flows, only grace from above may rule over one's soul. For His is the Power, the Glory now and forever.

As a child, we looked to the father and mother for food, security and direction. Would not a slave do the same? In good time we come into our own, and believe that we are the masters of our soul . . . so befalls us the vanity of man.

If left to believe that we are truly in control, survival itself would be a miracle against insurmountable odds that would be against us. Life without faith challenges the very purpose of the blessings we have received: feelings, reason, communication, logic, compassion, wisdom, love, dexterity, memories, understanding . . . such would these be without purpose, if not for the blessing of faith.

Freedom is never lacking as long as faith is preserved. Others may seek to control and remove these blessings from our lives, but they have, and always will, fail.

For he that is without faith in the Lord, lacks the freedom born of submission. They cannot take what which one has given up freely. No one can control he and that which he has pledged to the Lord.

As Jesus so commended his spirit unto the Father, no king, nor jury, nor soldier, nor sinner could control the Freedom that He alone possessed.

There is but one truth, and but one freedom to submit oneself to faith in our Lord and Savior.

September 2, 2001

In the Gathering of Faith

In the gathering of men
And women by their side
In a group of honest witness
All truth they cannot hide.

While in a place of worship
The children will refrain
As words of God are spoken
In the blessings of His name.

For whenever people gather
To correct a wrong they face
The words of wisdom spoken
Make this a holy place

In the gathering of people
Where honest words abound
We'll conquer life's great problems
And His wisdom will be found

September 6, 2001

The North Star

May your faith be as the North Star. Though seasons change, as do the evening skies, may the changes within thee revolve around thy faith.

Hearken not thy faith unto the new found beauty of a rising constellation, but anchor thy faith secure in the blessings of the Lord. For though great turmoil may come at the meeting of the waters, so shall thy faithful view of that which is constant see you through the tempest.

Anchor not thy soul unto the shifting sands of public debate, for beneath the surface such is a ship without a rudder in a tide of no clear direction.

Set sail instead on a mission of salvation, from where is found a true courage against the tides of evil men.

With the coast of one's own choosing, through the faithful council of the wise salvation is in sight, question not thy settings; and, as a lion seeks his portion through eyes in the dark of night, so shall thy sight leave not the guidance of the North Star.

"And remember that calm seas do not a seasoned sailor make."—**African Proverb**

September 7, 2001

The Winds of Change

From where do winds of change commence
On distance sands their waves dispense
The dunes give way on desert lands
As caravans cross, His guiding hands.

The winds of change pressed wood ships along
To worlds anew, a new sung song.
Of tales and beasts that stir one's fear.
The winds of change that brought us here.

When calm, a world that's found its peace
His love will conquer, our faith increased
Forever changed those winds prevail
With faith in Christ, we must make sail.

All journeys have an element of fear. For as life itself is a journey, there is no greater fear than that which is unknown. Perhaps that is why man's quest for discovery and knowledge is so great.

Just as Abraham, Mohammed, Moses, Mary and Joseph, the Disciples, and all the famous explorers of past crossed deserts, climbed mountains and set sail in turbulent times, today we continue this great tradition. We too set sail in winds of change. Casting all fears aside, we conquered flight, found means to live underwater for months at a time, explored the inner workings of our own bodies while pursuing solutions to our greatest fears . . . illness and death.

Throughout these journeys, in search of a scientific confirmation of the source of the winds of change, what have we learned? Oh, so much, for the search itself has opened so up much to mankind. New leaders and governments, new lands and new people, new methods and understandings, new cures, as well as, new ailments. Such is the journey of life. For as long as we search for the scientifically-defined source of the winds of change, life will be mystery. But as a blessing to the faithful followers, it will never be feared.

September 9, 2001

The Half Mast

Somewhere between the break of day
And the rise of the noonday sun
Today our flag is flying,
The "half mast" has just begun.

In three acts of senseless cowardice
Innocent lives today were lost
From the dust of destruction clamored
Never weighing risks or costs.

For those who shout in victory,
Voices deft to all our ears
American rescue workers are bravest
When fighting against one's fears

No matter what towers toppled,
Or planes or fortresses breached
The American foundation is strongest
Built on freedom found, and preached.

September 11, 2001

What Does it Mean to be American?

It is who one is, when freedom is found
It is what one does, when others need help
It is when people gather, in honest debate
It is where one is, in response to injustice
It is how one acts, when confronted with adversity
It is why all seek, to come to this land

September 13, 2001

In The Gathering

(A follow up to September 6th Poem)

Have you ever watched the dynamics of a group meeting? Even in the informal gathering various roles and positions emerge; the basis of which will determine the course to be taken and the eventual outcome, which will result.

Invariably a daring soul will initiate a welcome and statement of purpose, introductions will be heard, opinions will be made and references will be cited. Past events will be recounted, observations will be voiced, challenges will be expressed and debates will ensue.

If conducted with an honest, and yet compassionate, regard for the feelings of others, an open mind prevails, and the mission of the meeting is reached. Ideas exchanged meld together. Varying perspectives fine tune and direction is discovered.

It is a beautiful thing to watch. I have observed that the larger the group, and the greater the appearance of it becoming a lecture by one dominant individual, the longer the meeting. Less involvement by others tends to result in poorer content and a lack of common interest prevails.

This is where great speakers and leaders are born; those who have mastered the delivery of a sincere message, in a way that all who listens can relate; one whose words, inflections and feelings, can become one with the masses. As long as one maintains a compassion for all mankind, and fears the Lord, they will not get caught up in their own rhetoric.

September 14, 2001

A Senseless Act

How does one make sense of a senseless act? Where does one begin in defending such an ungodly sin? There is no rhythm or reason that we can comprehend in the actions taken against so many innocent lives. For such was the ultimate display of a growing evil against the greater good.

The respect for human life and the sufferings of life are but a mystery; for we all seek to attain, but seldom can maintain, an inner peace and harmony in our lives.

There are individuals and forces whose intentions are to capitalize on this fact, and in pursuit of their own vanity to achieve earthly power, become but pawns in the world of spiritual power.

For as surely as these terrorists' actions sought to forever disrupt an orderly and peaceful world, they have failed to inflict a critical blow to the spiritual world. The world of faith, love and compassion for others are now united. A common sense and purpose to preserve and expand humanity's greatest asset, compassion, has been brought back into our daily lives.

On that one single day, the world has witnessed together the power of true evil here on earth. From that day forward, however, the vision shared has stirred in each of us a spiritual focus as to how best respond to this senseless act . . . for only love conquers all. A new world within our hearts is now shared. With those who have died, with those who have suffered, with those who now pray. For those around the world with love and compassion in their hearts, we are now truly united.

May the blessings of humanity rise above senseless evil, now and forever.

September 15, 2001

Blessed is the Gathering

Grieve not for those who are now with Christ, for their suffering is no more. Though it be the dusk that warns of the darkness that lies ahead, it is truly not the end of the day. For the dusk of death is but the promise of a new eternal dawn with Christ.

Fear not my children, for thy Savior has removed the veil of darkness. There is a special light that he has left in your heart. It is warmed by the memories of lives so special; lives that were shared so honestly, completely and compassionately.

Such is that which we have shared with our fallen friends and neighbors, for it is they who have brought us together today; first to mourn, then to share fond memories, and forever to rejoice in the gift of their life eternal.

It is they who have touched us all. As in the words of our Savior, (Matthew 18:18) *Again I say unto you, That if two of you shall agree on earth as touching any thing that they shall ask, it shall be done for them of my Father which is in Heaven.*

19. For where two or three are gathered together in my name there am I in the midst of them.

These past few weeks, millions of people the world over have gathered together, hand-in-hand and heart-to-heart. We have all been touched by the stories of heroes, both living and now departed. The bond that has been created by these stories crosses over the great divide between us all.

We are truly humbled by these events and lives that are now so much a part of who we are. Take heart not to judge how others may deal with the stress and strains from these memories. Be mindful of the compassion they seek. Encourage them to help others, for such is healing unto oneself.

For blessed is the gathering.

In the name of the Father, the Son and the Holy Spirit, Amen.

September 27, 2001

Look into Their Windows

The most devastating of events has become an open window into who we are as Americans. The value of our daily lives has now become one of greater reflection, as to who we are, how we see others and what it means to be an American.

As so many people arose on that now fateful morning, who would have known of the events that would unfold.

There should be a monument to those who have fallen and those who have survived; one of who they were, and who we are, that can be shared. With the section of the World Trade Center that was saved, I thought that it would be appropriate to bring together the symbols of what we would most like to remember. For in this battle of good versus evil, the warriors were those who were trained all their lives to save innocent lives versus the terrorists who were trained to take innocent lives. Firemen, EMT's, Policemen, Security Guards, Military Personnel and Pilots should be remembered behind the windows that forever frame them in our memories. They are our heroes, one and all, dedicated to the preservation of life, liberty and the pursuit of happiness.

We've lost some of our nation's brightest and the best. From little children en route with their teachers, to the wife of politician and professionals of many industries have perished. The number of husbands, wives, sons and daughters, families, friends and acquaintances is multiplied now by how their stories affect our daily lives from that day forward.

> Look into their windows and see them as they worked.
> Look into their windows their duty never shirked.
> With loving hands they called home, to put our minds at rest
> Then on to help the others, humanity at it's best.

The fallen never faltered when charging through the gate
With character and commitment against these acts of hate.
Theirs' is but the glory. Let triumphant bells be tolled.
May the memories of these heroes, eternally unfold.

For every race and creed and color, every hope and dream and care.
Are all today but one heart, in the faith and love we share.

Look out through our windows, for they are windows on the world.
America the beautiful, a faithful flag unfurled.

October 1, 2001

A ship

... is a complicated vessel for travel. Having to deal with the currents, tides and waves below and the wind, storms and lightening above, a ship is in constant battle for control. In fact even when the elements are not against it, to move forward is an effort. In the absence of wind, currents or a rising or falling tide, a ship needs the power to move forward.

Such can be said for the human spirit, for it too is a complicated vessel. Housed within our sea of emotional feelings lies our spiritual craft; armed with the firm anchor of commitment to our Lord, His love was sent to us in the form of our Savior. For our faith in Jesus, is much like the trust that sailors must have in the rudder that will guide them home.

Our spiritual ship is outfitted with tall sails of our hope that can catch the winds of fortune to move us forward. The hull of our spiritual vessel is honed from strong timbers. Timbers of character, bound together with tenyons of faith; for faith is the bonding element that holds our entire spiritual vessel together.

When rough seas and torrential storms befall us, the sails of fortune must be drawn in, else they be ripped apart in the gale. A firm hand on the rudder and a keen eye on the buffeting waves is required. Though the planks and beams may shudder and strain under the brutality of confrontation with the elements, our faithful bonds will not falter.

Is this not where we are today? Have not the events of recent weeks challenged our innermost feelings to rise to the surface? Outward displays of compassion, camaraderie, unity, and patriotic pride has surfaced everywhere. Hidden for years beneath a dark sea of falsehoods, scandals, obsessive behavior, and the pursuits of worldly wealth, the true spirit of who we are as Americans has come to light.

Now, with our hands firmly on the rudder and our eyes looking out on the horizon of a sea of troubles, let us pull in our sails of fortune, secure our tenons of faith and regain control for the battles that lie ahead.

For when we, as true Americans, see our way through this tempest of terrorism, we shall once again way anchor, and hoist our sails of hope; a hope for a future that will recognize that which is truly important in our lives. And one that recognizes the needs of others here, and throughout the world, once again.

October 9, 2001

The Song of Calvary

How sweet the song of Calvary
That summons but our soul
The weight of wood, the blood that spilled
A hefty ransom, price and toll

To face the gate to heaven
Requires not deeds or good intentions
Our lives were bought before our birth
By His grace, let Christ be mentioned

The scriptures speak in volumes
What the Lord of Host has shared
Rejoice in jubilation
Our salvation now declared.

When rising in the morning
May a prayer come from your heart
Thanks to the Lord Almighty
We know now how to start

On a journey towards salvation
Let each step be strong and true
For the love that He's delivered
Reaches out to me and you.

October 14, 2001

One Leaf of All

Have you ever tried to find the most beautiful leaf of the autumn season? Walking along the rustling leaves, perhaps a yellow and green one will stand out, and as you bend down to pick it up, another beautiful red one will float by and catch your fancy. Standing with leaf in hand you claim, this it, and hold it up in the light to admire its color. But what is that? Behind your cherished find, way up on the tree above . . . could that be the most beautiful leaf?

Like the seasons that change, our time in the sun is but a fleeting moment. We capture the camera or microphone, and for those brief moments, whoever is watching or listening, they have focused on us.

Like that special leaf that was lifted into the sunlight, we are "the most beautiful leaf" ever discovered. The joy and excitement that we share with the admirer cannot be replaced. That is . . . until another floats by.

However, if one steps back; and closes their eyes before an autumn covered forest or mountain, and slowly opens their eyes but just a crack to let the light in, the most beautiful **leaf of all** will appear. It is the single image of all the leaves combined as one, spectacular in its variety of color and splendor.

I believe that this is what our Lord sees in us. The magic of a single creation cannot out shine all of creation.

Sometimes, however, we need to focus our attention to individuals. Sometimes we need to see the beauty and wonder of one to appreciate the splendor many. This truth could not have been more evident than the days following the events of September 11th.

For weeks now we have read, listened and watched the heroic stories of the lives of those who had fallen on that now fateful day. Our joy of discovery of what wonderful people they were, binds us all together in the tears that we now share with their families.

Like the search for the most beautiful leaf, this autumn I have discovered the greatest of our Lord's creations; in each and every one of us; for we are but one . . . one leaf of all . . . of God's love and creations.

Hold your life like a leaf up to God. Know that the life you have to offer is part of the most the beautiful one leaf of all. For all, not one, make an autumn what it is, beautiful.

October 23, 2001

For Lynne

When do you arise, my love?
At the song of the morning dove
When but one dove alone you see
Is when my Lord has come for me

Ours is a treasured gift of two
Sharing one life of love with you
For in you I find my bright of day
Forever with you is where I'll stay

We'll walk along on evening sand
On beaches cool, both hand in hand
No matter how far we'll be apart
My love will rest within your heart

For you are the true love of my life
In death, one finds but no more strife
That's why our time together is so dear
And why there's nothing left to fear

Find peace in the truth of words
Rest not with distrust or rely on swords
For the battles we fought are already won
When we chose to believe, God's holy Son

Though He comes to take me far away
There is so much more now left to pray
For I am yours and you are mine
Our love transcends both space and time

When next the morning you arise
Remember this and dry your eyes
"You are the greatest gift to me;
And, in everyone you meet and see:
Look deep within their eyes and find
A part of them that's wise and kind"

For in every heart that's touched by grace
There's unmistakable love found in their face
For that is what I found be true
In the beautiful love I found in you

November 1, 2001

A Way Back Home

When one plans a new venture, be it a vacation, a new business venture, or perhaps the pursuit of higher education, there is one thing that must hold true . . . you must have a home base.

A vacation is usually only a vacation if you are temporarily getting away from your home; a new business venture is often required if you are looking to build a better home; and a higher education is necessary if your looking to improve your home. So what exactly is a home?

As a child it is a place of security and comfort provided by your parents. As a traveler, it could be a temporary shelter under a tent or in a hotel. For the student it might be a fraternity or sorority house, or an apartment shared with friends.

Many say that a home is where the heart is; regardless of where you are, or where you're headed. To the refugee this must assuredly be true. Without permanent shelter, and moving from camp to camp, a home takes on a whole new meaning.

For one of the most important aspects of defining what a home is, it must be a place that you can return to. Be it the welcoming arms of a parent or loved one, or the office after a day of meetings to regroup one's thoughts, or the student housing to relax and prepare for one's studies. To the refugee it might be a shelter from the storm or simply the comfort of a warm blanket.

Our Lord has set for us a table. Our home is at His table that awaits us. No matter what the trials and tribulations that we endure here on this earth, His table does not differentiate one guest from another. For when we sit at His table, we are no longer guests, since we have returned home; for His is the heart of blessed assurance, and His arms are always opened for those who seek Him.

When you feel low, and oppressed by the weight of this world, and fear that you can't find your way back home, fear not and find refuge in these facts. For your home awaits you. It is safe. It is eternal. And through Jesus Christ, you have already been provided with a way back.

November 8, 2001

When My Savior Comes for Me

When my Savior comes for me
How ready I must be
For though it seems I've never cared
It's His love, that He, has always shared

In darkest moments when I have lied
His forgiveness is, what's sadly tried
When I sinned He took my hand
And lead toward a life so grand

How can I kneel before His grace
And seek forgiveness from His face
For His compassion knows no bound
The greatest sacrifice we've found

For by the blood He shed for me
On that hill at Calvary
Washed my sins and fears away
This is why this day I pray

May I pledge my life to Thee
Be it wealth or poverty
Matters not, how that I died
Matters most, how much I tried

November 9, 2001

To Judge Thee Not Guilty

How can it be that those who think we are not without sin find it in ourselves to try to judge others? We know that deep within our hearts there is little room to hold another's guilt, for ours is a vessel heavily laden with the guilt of our making.

Is it possible that finding fault in others somehow lessens our burden? If anything it should bring us closer, to know the guilt that we have created for ourselves has been created by and is shared with others now and before us.

Perhaps the next time you feel the urge to chastise someone for the shame that they may seem to be denying, we should look into the shadows of our own dark past, pull out a sin that we have denied and confess it to the One who judges not.

For Christ has written His response to those who confess their sins; with the blood of salvation, His response is not guilty. For the One who is pure of heart and yet knows first hand the challenges and temptations that we must face in this life, also knows of the salvation that awaits those who judge not others.

Thanks be to God, for He who comes to judge the quick and the dead, has blessed us with a Savior and a way to righteousness.

November 10, 2001

Wisdom

Wisdom is an interesting word. A derivation of wise and kingdom, it suggests a place of peaceful knowledge.

But if one is knowledgeable, is not one aware of the evils and problems of man? And knowing the evils of the world, how can one be peaceful? If one is full of knowledge, should not their failure to resolve the problems tear at their inner peace?

Perhaps a wise person has two other attributes. Perhaps wisdom can only begin when one has faith and understanding. No matter how much knowledge one achieves, one will never know all that there is to life. That domain rests with One, and only One.

When one recognizes this and acknowledges that *we stand beneath Him, understanding* is born. When one confesses their inability to resolve a problem and places their faith with the Lord, wisdom can begin to flourish. For when we say that "we do not understand," we suggest that we are no longer beneath He that does.

The wise man knows that he will always understand . . . through his faith in the glory of The Almighty, he will find his peace in the kingdom of God.

Praise be to the Lord, and the wisdom that He grants those through faith and understanding.

November 16, 2001

Romancing The Stars

What is romance
To the innocent mind
Is it something that's missing
And so hard to define

Of all the compassions
And feelings expressed
The romance with another
Can't be equaled or best

On the beach with waves crashing
Or lying close by my side
These feelings of romance
I can no longer hide

For ours is romance
Be we near or be far
Bring warmth this cold morn
As we watch shooting stars

These are the moments
When romance is defined
Catching visions together
In our hearts and our minds

Since our wishes were granted
By the love that we've shared
With the next star that's sighted
Let us wish what we dare

That our son may discover
Who his true love will be
By the romance that he sees
Between you and between me

November 17, 2001

A Village Thanksgiving

In Weeden's Park under the chestnut tree
On the bench a squirrel sits and awaits for me
To the left there's a gazebo down a short gravel trail
Behind is the post office where we all get our mail

In this village there are many at the break of dawn
Picking up the morning papers on the front yard lawn
As the cafe and the bagel shops set up the sidewalk chairs
Traditions and Euphorbia display their country wares

The lawyers and the architects join bankers and dignitaries
Across the street the church bell rings, as two other loves are married

These are the morning sights and sounds of a town called Lawrenceville
Three hundred years it's been this way; let's pray that it always will

November 22, 2001

A Way Back Home

When one plans a new direction, be it a vacation, a new business venture, or perhaps the pursuit of higher education, there is one thing that must hold true . . . you must have a home base.

A vacation is usually only a vacation if you are temporarily getting away from your home; a new business venture is often required if you are looking to build a better home; and a higher education is necessary if you're looking to improve your home. So what exactly is a home?

As a child it is a place of security and comfort provided by your parents. As a traveler, it could be a temporary shelter under a tent or in a hotel. For the student it might be a fraternity or sorority house, or an apartment shared with friends.

Many say that a home is where the heart is. Regardless of where you are, or where you're headed. To the refugee this must assuredly be true. Without permanent shelter, and moving from camp to camp, a home takes on a whole new meaning.

For one of the most important aspects of defining what a home is, it must be a place that you can return to. Be it the welcoming arms of a parent or loved one, or the office after a day of meetings to regroup one's thoughts, or the student housing to relax and prepare for one's studies. To the refugee it might be a shelter from the storm or simply the comfort of a warm blanket.

Yes, a home is where the heart is. Regardless of where you are, or where you're headed. It is a refuge for the weary.

Our Lord has set for us a table. Our home is at His table that awaits us. No matter what the trials and tribulations that we endure here on this earth, His table does not differentiate one guest from another. For when we sit at His table, we are no longer guest, but we have returned home. For His is a heart of blessed assurance; and His arms are always opened for those who seek Him.

When you feel low, and oppressed by the weight of this world, and fear that you can't find your way back home, fear not and find refuge in these facts. For your home awaits you. It is safe. It is eternal. And through Jesus Christ, you have already been provided with . . . a way back.

A Need Unknown

If you've ever had to wear corrective lenses, you know the frustration of having to adjust. The ability to focus clearly under varying circumstances, be it light, distance, size of text or movement is a constant challenge. And of course, there is always the insult to injury if you've ever misplaced your glasses. For to find what you need, is what you need to find.

Isn't this one of life's greatest ironies? To find what you need . . . is what you need to find. Perhaps the answer is not in the discovery, but in the quest. For once you find what you need, do you need it any longer?

Sometimes I feel that this is a fundamental premise in any successful capitalist society . . . the quest to fulfill a need; particularly at this time of year, when the holidays are filled with commercials of what we must have, or where we must be and what we must do.

There is a lot of need out there, and there are many who want to convince us of what it is we need. Or share their vision of what it all means.

Corrective vision; Muhammad saw the mountain. Moses was drawn to a burning bush. And Buddha beheld the beauty of nature.

Centuries ago, shepherds and kings saw a special star in the sky. All followed this vision in search of a need undefined, a quest unknown. But upon its discovery, their need became their quest. For they all chose to make it a part of their daily lives and share all that they had discovered with the world.

Wise men brought gifts to our Savior. They had no prior knowledge of what their king would need, but what they discovered was far greater. To find what they needed, they needed to find salvation.

Peace, harmony and a way unto the Lord of infinite understanding.

Is this not what we all seek this and most every holiday season? A vision of infinite understanding when around the world Ramadan, Chanukah, Christmas and many celebrations are occurring. Cultures and religions are celebrating what they needed to find. Peace, harmony and a way unto the Lord of infinite understanding.

Perhaps this will be the year of discovery. Enjoy the search for the perfect gift. Don't be frustrated by the blurred vision of flashing lights. Put on your corrective lenses of what you need to find.

And perhaps what you will find will include peace in the smile of a child waiting in line to see Santa; harmony to be found in the holding of hands at the blessing of the end of a daily fast, understanding in the lighting of a candle, be it Advent or Hanukkah. Joy in the understanding that all over the world people like you and me are celebrating: the fulfillment of a need unknown in our minds; but at home in our hearts.

This year I would like to wish the world the happiness of the holidays: the blessings of peace, the harmony of friendship and the understanding of love.

December 5, 2001

A Place of Prayer, Pride and Purpose

We recently traveled by train to New York City with our son and one of his friends. With no particular purpose but to see the sights, have dinner and enjoy the beginning of the holiday season, we set out from the train station at Hamilton, New Jersey.

The ride was peaceful as the train slowly filled with each new stop where one was hard pressed to see anyone leave. Arriving in Penn Station, we disembarked into the depths of the underground. I marveled at the calm of the passengers as we were corralled into narrow walkways along the tracks between stairs that were temporarily closed for renovation.

While waiting in the concourse under Madison Square Garden I was greeted by a good friend and neighbor who, with his son, was en route to the Wake Forest basketball game. I commented on his early arrival to which he replied they were going to visit the World Trade Center site before the game.

Winding our way up Seventh Avenue we realized that we might have picked the worst day since it was the day after Thanksgiving. But like many around us, it was a special day to be thankful. Referred to as "Black Friday" unbeknownst to me at the time, this was to be a day to pay our respects and enjoy the blessings of life.

We walked through Times Square, strolled through Bryant Park, and had drinks in the Marriott Marquis. We were sorry to discover that the tree at Rockefeller Center would not be lit until the following week. Standing majestically above the golden statue and the ring of ice skaters below, nestled between the towering buildings, it was still a grand sight to behold. Afterwards we stopped by St. Patrick's Cathedral to light a candle, then moved on to enjoy a dinner just off Broadway.

When we left the restaurant, I had made a wrong turn in our journey back toward the station. Walking by a construction site we came upon banners, posters and then flowers as we came up to Engine House 54, Ladder #4. Surrounded by messages of condolences and photos of the brave brothers lost on September 11, we realized that we had not made a wrong turn after all. I spoke to fireman for a few moments after Lynne had pointed out a poster-size message from a small town in Pennsylvania, Canonsburg.

This was the place to leave the three prayers and perspectives that I had been carrying in my pocket should we ever make it to Ground Zero that day. Lynne had bought a rose to which I tied a prayer; another I tied to the post of a small American flag and the last was affixed onto a pipe on the firehouse; a place of prayer, a place of pride and a place of purpose.

A few blocks later we came upon a sculpture. Caught up in customs, the delayed delivery of this tribute to fallen fireman was resting on a small trailer just off the curb. The bronze figure from a European artist had a candle, flower and prayer before him. It was a good day to be in New York. It was good place to be, indeed.

A place of prayer, pride and purpose
These blessings I hold dear
For though evil seeks to triumph
From this place we shall not fear

For those who care so deeply
And rush in to save the others
They will never be forgotten
And forever be our brothers.

A place of prayer, pride and purpose
May this house be always blessed
Through the blessings of this nation
May these brothers lie at rest.

December 7, 2001

The "I" Beam of Democracy

One of the greatest creations in the construction industry was the I-beam. Steel in the form of the letter "I" bears so many qualities. In addition to its strength and durability, the three sides provide ample surface and flexibility to attach and protect other materials necessary to erect bridges, massive structures and towering skyscrapers.

A whole new world of creations started here, in Trenton, New Jersey. From a small building on the Delaware River, the Roebling plant also designed and engineered suspension bridges made of steel and cables.

But the I-beam is only useful once it is joined with another I-beam. This is what the good man does. He brings together those who can connect with a clear purpose: those who will unite, for a shared vision; the ones, who in a heroic effort to save others, become a circle of friends, and say, "let's roll." The same persons who are willing to risk it all to become the people; the "I's" who will bond together to become "we."

As with the American Revolution, America was born again in the era of the industrial revolution. The I-beam was a key factor then, as it still is today. And with the recent tragedies on our beloved American soil, it may be more important now, than ever.

When the World Trade Center and Pentagon were attacked, images that I will never forget were the massive I-beams exposed in Washington and the piles-upon-piles of I-beams tangled together in New York. For all of the lives that were lost, few human bodies were left intact. But the I-beams, they somehow remained.

I am sure that as the days unfold, and new stories of those who lost their lives emerge, we will come to see how important each and every one of us is to each other. As the tragic images fade and the I-beams are removed, we will reflect and be thankful for those who brought us together.

The architects and engineers of the American Revolution who crafted a new form of governing were followed by those who designed and built this nation's great cities and industries. And today, as the information age begins a new era for us and our children to follow, let us be mindful of the contributions of others. To support in times of sorrow, to comfort in times of pain. To respond to acts of terror, and rebuild in times of peace; for we are the I-beams of this great Democracy, and together we shall bind together, and endure.

December 12, 2001

The Christmas Gift

As shepherds slept a star appeared, before the Angels' came. In journeys walked the wearied cried. A time when fear once ruled the night; a gift was sent to set it right.

A child was born in Bethlehem. Three kings knew not what they sought; a Savior from the wicked. Wise men with gifts they brought.

For within our hearts' desire, there's a void that must be filled. Make a manger in your heart. Let your cares and woes be stilled.

On this day when Christ was born, in the heavens the angels sang. The One prophets knew would come: our Lord's gift to us, His Son.

December 23, 2001

A Manger in Your Heart

Build a manger in your heart; a place where peace is born again. Where the wearied travelers may find comfort; and the oppressed a safe haven from the dark.

Fill your heart with the warmth of salvation that comes from sharing your home with others. Welcome those from afar, as you treasure the ones you love so near.

Build a manger in your heart.
And His peace will come to stay. Where no other room is found,
May His love abound, we pray.

December 23, 2001

Forgive Us Our Debts

It is a hard concept to grasp. Possibly because we know how many debts we owe to others. Or, perhaps, because we have failed to forgive debts that we feel are owed to us by others. But in the Lord's Prayer, we seek the greatest blessing of all from the One to whom we owe our greatest debt.

He provides for us *our daily bread and leads us not into temptation, but delivers us from evil.* Yet do we not fail to give thanks at the dinner table? And do we not lead ourselves to the temptations of sin around us every day? When evil has befallen us, to whom do we immediately turn to for deliverance . . . He who is without sin; He who is full of grace.

Our debts in life are many. If one is to seek the forgiveness of one's debts one must be prepared for a genuine commitment to duty. There is a fine line of distinction between one's responsibilities and one's duties. Yet our debts are as numerous as the stars that light a clear evening sky.

We must all be held accountable to our responsibilities. A parent is responsible to care for the health and welfare of their child. A student is responsible for completion of their studies and assignments. A laborer is responsible for the movement of material or supplies. For a debt of gratitude is owed to the parent by a child who is healthy and of good heart. To the teacher of a student who's success is born of diligence and knowledge. Between both master and loyal laborer who both recognize their indebtedness to each other. But it is our duty to treat each other with respect kindness.

We hold these truths to be self evident that all men are created equal. The true balance of mankind is found in how we chose to treat others. Kindness cannot exist but for the recognition of our equality. The measure of a man is not by what he has achieved in life, as seen by others, but by the kindness he has shown to himself, by how he chooses to treats others.

As long as man places himself above the laws of nature, the Word of our Lord and seeks denial of our equality, mankind will be cursed with spiritually bankrupt leaders like Hitler and Bin Laden who, in desperate acts of denial, seek to destroy mankind through acts of genocide and terrorism.

The boundaries of man do not exist in the eyes of our Lord. *His will be done*, regardless of the barriers set by men of such evil intent. No cave or concentration camp wall can keep Him out or hold men of faith hostage within. The debts that cannot be forgiven are those against mankind.

As stated by our President, "whether or not they are brought to justice, or justice is brought to them, justice will be done" so shall the will of our Lord be done. We shall be delivered from evil, and our debts shall be forgiven.

January 2, 2002

Among the Faithful in the Followers

The past eight months of personal experiences working in the city of Trenton have me reminiscing of my childhood visits to downtown Pittsburgh in the sixties. Our father would walk us through cavernous skyscrapers that he leased while pointing out the historic and architecturally significant structures that were worthy of preservation.

On East State Street, nestled between the Department of Taxation and across from my building stands a decaying brick colonial. A few blocks away, a spectacular stone structure houses The Department of Revenue. Above its entrance, a wrought iron silhouette of a worker and on the turret roof a ship at sail serves as a weathervane.

These images and memories are a comfort when one considers the recent events that have shattered our sense of safety and belief in the future.

In one's lifetime we faithfully follow many before us. In a family, it could be our parents or grandparents. At work, our instructors or teachers. Early on in life, our predecessors are where we look for guidance, yet in our faith for the future, those who follow is where we must focus our attention; especially in our later years.

How wonderful it is to discover that there is one who has followed you throughout your life. One who knows your success, has seen your failures, was there when you rejoiced and shared in your deepest sorrows.

He is that child within. She is the kind hearted soul. They are sons and daughters who will take the torch of faith, and like the Olympic runners will span the globe, and pass it from person to another. From one generation to the next; the eternal flame of the faithful followers.

This is what our Lord does for us. He not only leads, but He too follows us. Like the patient parent behind a wobbling toddler taking their first steps. Through the years of our competing toward the next goal we've set, He is our most vocal cheerleader. To loving care giver in the nursing home, whose arms lift us to a gentle rest, our Lord follows us . . . protects us, cheers us on and in the end, delivers us.

> Among the faithful in the followers is where our Lord is found
> In the bustle and the hoopla there is nary but a sound
> Listen closely to the footsteps of the one who walks behind
> Among the faithful in the followers is where our Lord you'll find.

January 11, 2002

In One's Best Interest

Have you ever marveled at the growth of a tree? Year in and year out, it slowly inches upward and outward through all kinds of conditions. As seasons change, a tree adjusts. And recently, scientific studies have proved that trees in a cluster or forest emit varying chemicals into the soil through their roots to communicate with each other.

How different is a tree's growth from our own? What decisions must a tree make that are not unlike that of a child?

Through each season, as throughout one's life, conditions change. The angle of the sunlight shifts as the earth circles the sun. Some seasons are warmer or drier than others. Sometimes a bountiful rain is followed by an unseasonable draught.

Such events are true in the life of a child. The happiness of a family holiday can precede the gloom of returning to work or paying bills. Unexpected events such as the loss of a parent can place difficult decisions before an adolescent unseasonably soon; before they have had a chance to mature.

Not unlike the growing tree, a child must choose which way to branch out: toward the light, or away from the light. Perhaps the fulfillment of dreams entices the child to keep growing in one direction; or if pain or anguish was found in that direction, they may continually grow away from it. But as for the young sapling and the child within us, all seasons change, and in our own best interest we must seek to change with them, and branch out in many directions.

Well rounded, balanced and in perfect form, even the grandest tree must shed branches from time to time. In order to keep itself healthy, and allow other branches a chance to grow. So it is true for us. In our own best interest, we too must sometimes shed the branches of our past from time to time.

And now that we know that trees can communicate, we know that they are not alone. The tallest redwood forests actually have very shallow roots, yet they tower over others from a complex system of interlocking roots. Roots that not only nurture and feed the leaves in the canopy far above, but structurally support the massive trunks below. They rely on each other for strength, support and life. When one is removed the system is weakened, but the resolve is strengthened as new sapling work their way up through the roots of those around them.

Here again we discover the importance of what is in one's best interest. For a redwood will never reach its full potential alone. And every tree, as every person, cannot survive by only growing toward rewarding conditions or growing away from problems. Sometimes one must simply shed the weight of the past in pursuit of one's own future.

In one's best interest is not always an easy route to grow. But always remember, that in one's best interest, one is never alone.

January 12, 2002

A Journey Within

How often do we discuss the events of the day through the eyes of the mass media? In America the media has great power and with it comes the responsibility to decipher the facts from the fiction. Even if successful in the presentation, the interpretation rests with the reader.

These days, there are ample newsworthy topics for healthy discussion, be one at work, en-route or over a morning cup of coffee. And this hasn't change since the beginning of time.

How interesting it must have been in the days that our Savior walked this earth. News by word of mouth adds such a much greater personal quality. Unfettered by concerns over how one may misinterpret the written word, in biblical days, the spoken word carried an emotional quality that could be deemed politically incorrect these days.

In today's society there is a much more skeptical approach to the written word, and the stories that make the news tend to reflect that fact.

But every once in while, a great event occurs. Be it disaster or blessing, it cannot be ignored, and the spoken word is resurrected.

Such was the case in the days of our Lord. People mulled over His statements around the community well, outside synagogues and in private at home.

A new understanding surfaced by the simple eloquence of His parables; miracles that He performed threatened the disbelievers and encouraged those of little faith.

Today I travel to a site that survived the devastation of the World Trade Center disaster. Here again a major event of almost unprecedented proportion has people talking and taking that journey within. The reflection of emotions that have been buried deep within, under countless stories of scandals, corruption and general misdealing of mankind.

Like the pilgrims of generations past, we are willing to journey afar in search of a peace within. We are open to outward expressions of that which we repressed for fear of misinterpretation. Openness and honesty are once again at center stage.

Compassion and forgiveness have once again survived the endangered species list. A reprieve for the weary who have championed the cause of brotherhood: those who stood out against the injustice. Those whose fame is just as much a headline by what they didn't befall to as what they chose to stand against.

If these were the times that will test men's souls; then, blessed be fact that we have rediscovered a reason for the journey within.

January 15, 2002

The Vision We Seek

Dear Lord, we lift up our eyes searching for a vision. Deprived of the glory of meeting thy Son in the flesh, we long for a forgiveness that we might know in our heart. We cherish the Word as spoken by He who loves us more dearly that we could ever imagine. And must come to terms with our own shortcomings and those we choose to judge.

But in thy Word we find guidance. A vision that is clear and uncluttered. What we sought in the flesh we discover in the Word. Your Son's voice resonates with compassion, stands firm against evil, teaches through parables and compels us to help others.

Oh, that which we seek with a vision is not lost to blind. The pilgrimage of His blessings we walk toward is not out of step to the lame. The salvation we seek here in life is secured by our faith in a Savior through death.

His is the vision that lasts, and we are His image on earth. Let us honor our Lord, and see in each other, the vision we seek.

Amen

January 23, 2002

The Endless Gift

The love of the Lord is an endless gift
That will never leave your side
Waiting to be opened at every trial
It is the truth that He'll never hide

When the will is weak but the faith is strong
And you know not where to turn
By His guiding hand and His tender love
On that day you will surely learn

Of the patient heart and the peaceful mind
That will come from His promised gift
All your cares and woes with your faith let go
And your spirit He will surely lift

January 31, 2002

There is a Peace to be Found

There is a peace to be found; a moment of calm, when one's worries are of little regard. It is an elusive discovery that seems further from our reach when ever we seek it. But like the comforting touch of a loved one's hand, the smile of passing stranger or the soft crisp smell of fresh linens when you retire for the night . . . it is there.

Journey with me, if you will, to a distant memory; perhaps it is a place, an island or a rocky mountain. Maybe it is the feel of warm sand under your feet as you venture out on toward the crashing waves. The smell of the cocoa in the suntan lotion and the sea salt that blend together, just as you remembered as a child. And now it is your child who frolics in the waves and shouts for joy as your spouse lifts him above the waves or rests her into the foaming tidal pools.

Above, the laughing sea gulls' chatter is almost indistinguishable from the sounds of the other beach goers. But for now, the warm sun has relaxed your muscles as you soon drift off to sleep.

Peace is found. You are content and untroubled. You are not alone, and yet, you are somewhere far from the others around you. God has found you at home. It is His house where you feel most at ease. It is your home that awaits you in your hour of greatest need; for He will watch over you this day, for there is a peace to be found.

February 4, 2002

Partakers of Grace

Throughout the centuries man has attempted to dominate with power and influence over others. The ability to remove joy, control emotions, instill fear or take a life has been considered by many to be a power. I suggest otherwise, and the witness that I must defer to by way of example is the apostle Paul.

Picture if you will this scene of Paul, an older fellow stooped and balding while seated on the floor, chained by hand and feet. Towering over him is a Roman officer. In this dingy house, in a drab little room, he writes. He writes a letter, that two thousand years later you find. This letter from Paul is not of grievance, but of immeasurable joy.

Paul writes to Paul and Timotheus, to the servants of Jesus Christ, that **"grace *be* unto you, and peace."** Paul writes every prayer of his being made with joy for others; alone but for one capture by his side, He writes of "fellowship"; a fellowship in the gospel.

In the next line, Paul mentions "confidence" of this very thing **that he which hath begun a good work in you will perform it until the day of Jesus Christ.** At a time when one would justifiably feel fear and insecurity of one's next breath being one's last . . . Paul writes of confidence; being confident of this very thing.

To the on-looker one might describe this scene of one of shame and pity, but how does Paul describe his plight, in the next verse. He writes of having those he loves in his heart, and knowing that they too share in his plight, **"inasmuch as both in my bonds, and in defense and confirmation of the gospel, ye all are partakers of my grace."**

Where others might see a scene of shame and pity . . . Paul knows the grace of our Lord. His is the power over man, and His grace cannot be bound. His joy cannot be contained. His love cannot be restricted . . . For later on, Paul's letter continues: **"And this I pray, that your love may abound yet more and more in knowledge and *in* all judgment."**

That which binds the flesh cannot shackle one's faith. The spirit within is stronger than the power of the oppressor. We know these things to be true . . . but what of joy and grace?

To find "joy" in knowing that one's suffering is a part of the good work of that which he hath begun in you and is performing until the day of Jesus Christ.

To see "grace" in the defense and confirmation of the gospel through bondage, our friend Paul speaks of a greater freedom that is found in the defense and confirmation of the gospel . . .
shared with all who are now partakers of his grace, and through our knowledge of this letter, two thousand years later, and by the love in our hearts and prayers . . . we are now caretakers of the Word of God.

February 9, 2002

Written after reading **"A Letter of Joy"** from *Grace for the Moment* by Max Lucado

The Threshold of Compassion

Where do you think the greatest compassion can be found? Is it in the church; or at a family reunion, baptism or birthday?

Walk if you will amongst those in the waiting room of a hospital. It matters not be you on the maternity floor or outside an intensive care unit, for in either place you will find God's greatest compassion in the heart's of others.

Whether one comforts a loved one in their last moments, or cradles a new life, the sharing of one's soul to another cannot be denied here. A transition occurs, and like the threshold of a doorway, a life will enter one world as it leaves another.

Greetings and farewells are strongest in the waiting room of a hospital. Joy and sorrow are of paramount importance here; and afterwards, a new life begins for all who have waited so long.

I recall a sermon that spoke of Jesus, as a young carpenter. After a long day of working with His father, He stops in the doorway and out-stretching His arms, He recounts that He knows why His Father has sent Him.

Joseph watches as the setting sun casts his son's shadow, with arms out-stretched, over the wooden casket behind him. And Joseph now knows the compassion of the Lord that one finds in the threshold.

Watch for the thresholds in life; for there are many. Be it the father who is seeking gainful employment, or the spouse who is leaving an abusive household. Or perhaps, our sons and daughters as they graduate from high school and embark on the greatest journey of life. There are many thresholds between the waiting rooms of this life and eternal life that awaits us. Thanks to the mission of a young carpenter before us, the doorway is open and we need but seek the compassion to welcome others through its passing.

February 19, 2002

The Limit of One's Horizon

What is the horizon, but a line where one can discern of that which we can see and that which we cannot. Comprehension is similarly a barrier which must be breached between that which we know and that which we seek to understand.

Throughout life one may see many horizons, but they will not vary but for the weather and seasons if one fails to move on.

How different is the life of the fly that lives for a day and must condense all their experiences within 24 hours from the monarch butterfly that migrates thousands of miles, over land and oceans. The beauty that they each behold is but a reflection of the life they lead, and is outwardly expressed in the beauty they can share with others.

As you venture out this day in search of a greater understanding and comprehension of life, look to the horizon, and appreciate the beauty of the sunset. For as life moves on, so should you in search of new horizon's. And like the butterfly that must struggle to break free of the cocoon that has long protected it from harm, so must you now face new struggles that will strength your wings so that you too may fly on, over many lands and oceans, for many years.

And the beauty that we shall behold in you will be but a reflection of the life that you chose to lead. And the horizons of life, will once again, bear no limits.

February 17, 2002

St. Paul's Trinity Church

There's a cloud over the heart, and though it cannot be seen, its presence cannot be denied.

Sometimes events of great magnitude can change the perception of a whole nation, if not the entire world.

What is a "Day-in-Infamy" to us is but a passing grain of sand in the cosmos of a billion galaxies throughout all eternity to our Lord; and yet, through the love of His Son, He grieves with us. The prayers of all are heard. He turns not His back to us in our moment of sorrow; but lifts the cloud within to let us press on.

The compassion He offers is shared, abundantly.

While volunteering at St. Paul's Trinity Church in New York City, one can only marvel at the outpouring of sentiments sent from all over the world. Young students stopped to write messages of love and support to those who daily search to find those who perished. Letters, postcards, flags, handkerchiefs, pictures, flowers, origami, and other sentiments of prayers, faith and support adorn the gates, columns, walls, pews and windows of this small refuge for the weary. "Ground Hero" can be found on shirts dedicated to the rescue workers, firemen, EMT's and others who stormed in.

The oldest, continually operated public building in Manhattan, built in 1766, St. Paul's stands today among the wreckage and desolate empty buildings. On a small piece of land of what is termed "ground zero" the St. Paul's steeple stands tall.

Like the grain of sand, which was once unnoticed in the immense universe of space and time, this Trinity Church, stands today as a portal between the Father, the Son and Holy Spirit that survives in us all.

Fear not that your warm wishes and compassion for others may go unnoticed. For as I watched the smile of a fireman reading your letter, and the tears of those who stand arm-in-arm in line along the gate, or observe the silent reverence of crowds on the observation platform . . . your presence is known. And your love will help lift the cloud.

February 26, 2002

The Tracks We Leave and Follow

If you've ever lived or spent much time in the country, most likely you will have come across a set of tracks, be it in the snow or soil. A lot can be determined by the tracks that one leaves behind; not only the direction, but the speed by one's stride, or the reactions to events or conditions around one.

Archeologists have become masters at deciphering the most information about events of the past from tracks and conditions that surrounded them. Like a good mystery novel, hypothetical scenarios are explored, tested and reviewed again and again with a critical eye.

But how often in life do we take the time to look back at our own tracks? Are we pleased with where they've led us, or would we prefer to cover our tracks? Do they reflect good judgment when facing obstacles in our path? Did we learn from the decisions we made, or did we repeat them, only to end up where we started, or once again do they lead us into dyer straights?

There is a photo on this month's calendar in our home. It is of a beautiful sunset or sunrise, where drifting sand is in the foreground, a gently rolling grass plain in mid view, and striking mountains off in the distance. The contrast of these three varying conditions is accented by the tracks of three deer leading out before the observer.

Two tracks are side-by-side and third parallels on the left, a few feet away in the soft sand. About mid way across the sand, the two tracks cross at a point where the third deer comes closer to the other tracks. Beyond this point in the sand, the third deer's tracks lead off to the left, away and over the ridge out of sight, as the other two continue onward in the direction they had chosen.

How unlike the story of life do these tracks represent the families of man when parent's journey day in and out in search of pastures to feed and rest. Though obstacles, like the shifting sands beneath their feet or the distant mountains that loom ahead. They may slow them down, but they press on.

And if they are fortunate, a child or two will journey with them. Listening, learning and even leading so that when the time is right, they too, will bid their farewells and journey off as their parents had once before . . . at another time and in another place to be repeated in the tracks we leave in the sands of time.

March 6, 2002

They Knew Him Not

They knew Him not for why He came
And saw Him not, He was the same
The Son of God among the poor
A saving Grace, the One . . . the sure

In early morn they walked the earth
At setting sun their ship they berthed
Disciples twelve that dwelt with Him
Relinquished all gave not to sin

The faithful followers sought His word
Yet once condemned no cries were heard
He knew the path His Father set
Feared not the fate that He had met

With loving hands He healed the lame
On bloody nails would hang the same
With open arms He welcomes all
Who hear the Word and heed the call

This Easter morn no grave will hold
The sting of death as He had told
Rise up all faithful who now do know
Celebrate His life where 'ere you go!

March 17, 2002

A Prayer for the Weary

When the day is done, and it's time to retire; and, your eyes are about to close, no matter what the day has brought, be at peace with world.

And when you awake in the morning, be thankful to the Lord. For the one He loves will find favor in thy prayers. For this day is but the beginning of a new life for the weary.

A new life to be discovered on a new day, met with peaceful rest, a thankful heart and a loving Father, for the one He loves.

Blessed be our Savior and the loving Father who art in heaven. Amen

March 21, 2002

The Ritual of Recovery

The ritual of recovery
When fallen friends are found
The silent solemn victory
When walking on this ground.

These lives they sought to save
Both innocent and brave
With lines we light their passing
Out from this gravel grave.

A brotherhood are they
Though victims are we all
When beckoned to the grave
They answered evil's call

With strength and self conviction
With love and honesty
These fallen brothers' sought not
Fortune, fame or revelry.

These hallowed grounds within a canyon
The towering edifices we see
With whispered prayers in line we honor
The victory of recovery.

April 2, 2002

Thresholds & Archways

A Morning Prayer

He rises with the light of day. Where we venture out in trepidation, He steps forward in confidence. We question the sins we see in others, oblivious to our own reflection. His sight sees through all that seek to hide.

We rise from the dark of night; from that which we have done, and toward that which we will do. For His is the knowledge exposed from where we've come; when we chose to open our hearts.

Fear not the morning; be it brilliantly bright or fearfully dark, for His is the day that retreats not unto turmoil.

No greater love than He who shares your concerns is He who has walked before and He who has faced our greatest fears for us. He who has chosen to walk again, with you who have sought Him, and by He who knows what fate lies ahead.

Blessed is the journey that awakens unto truth. Blessed are thee whose pain and suffering knows the glory of Christ. For thy burden is not carried alone, but bears witness to your love and His compassion.

Awaken thy sleeping heart. And step forward, and be blessed.

Amen

April 5, 2002

The Mile and the Mill Stones

Celebrations are wonderful events. The planning and preparation can be almost as exciting as the event itself, if one's heart is truly into the effort.

Such can said be for the present moment. Consider the moments in life when either a milestone or a millstone are present. The former could be before you or the later a weight around your neck.

When there is a milestone in one's life, an anniversary, birthday, or holiday, how we chose to prepare mentally or emotionally will be reflected in the celebration, itself.

"Sow to yourselves in righteousness, reap in mercy; break up your fallow ground: for it is time to seek the Lord, till He come and rain righteousness upon you." HOSEA 10:12

The fallow ground cannot remain so, if one is to celebrate. The mundane repeat of daily life needs to be broken, so that one can sow compliments and reap happiness, when it is time to celebrate.

And yet there are times when a millstone seems to have weighed heavily around our neck; a burdensome weight that we have carried which needs to be lifted.

"Ye have plowed wickedness, ye have reaped inequity; ye have eaten the fruits of lies: because thou didst trust in thy way, in the multitude of thy mighty men." HOSEA 10:13

Our Lord knows all, sees all and nothing about us can be hidden from our Creator. When we chose to trust in our way, or totally in the way of our leaders without the benefit of counseling with our Lord, we chose to "eat the fruit of lies."

Recent accounts of executives who plowed wickedness while all who reaped supposed wealth, it was "unequal." For so many, it was but wealth that was on paper only: the fruit of lies from the wicked chosen by the innocent; some without conscious, or others without proper counsel.

But it all has been exposed. And our discovery of the truth gives good cause to celebrate. For now we know of what was sown, and what was reaped. It is time to break up our fallowed ground once more. We must sow to ourselves in righteousness and prepare to reap in mercy.

Leadership requires many skills and talents; a delicate balance between many factors. If one is surrounded by men and women of good conscious, kind hearts and strong wills much can be accomplished. The millstone becomes not a burden, but is a tool, as originally intended: a tool of strength and character building for a stronger individual.

And as for the milestone, let it not become a depressing image of time and its passing, but a goal to be reached, passed and sighted again.

In these two verses of Hosea 10, verses 12 and 13, I have found the blessing of "perspective." Life comes with many milestones and millstones. How we chose to perceive them is up to us.

April 16, 2002

Through the Garden Gate

One enters by His way

When my wife and I traveled to Edinburgh for our twentieth anniversary, we marveled at the beautiful gardens in the city. Below Edinburgh Castle, in the long valley between the new city and the old city were roses and flowers that highlighted the hills, one must traverse steep steps to enjoy that which waits below.

The park was inviting as one leaves the noise and pollution of the bustling streets above. In the constant presence of the castle, which overlooked all in every direction, one could find a sense of peaceful respite. Set in the hillside was a monument dedicated to the brave people and soldiers who fought for freedom, and further down the path one finds a beautiful carousel whose melodies echoed the sound of children's laughter and delight.

Later in the day we enjoyed buying our lunch from a small bakery back in a residential part of the city. While looking for a spot to picnic, we came upon a beautiful fenced park, where we roamed in search of a gate. Once discovered, we found it to be locked, and although we could see others inside, none would open it for us. Later we recalled reading how Edinburgh has neighborhood gardens which are fenced in and gated for only local residents use.

No matter, for a bench found at the side steps of wonderful stone church across the street served us well, and a healthy lunch was enjoyed.

Today my thoughts drift back to that wonderful day, and I remember how disappointed I was to not enter the garden. Tired, hungry and craving a place to rest from our long walk, the wrought iron gate was all that was between us, and that which we sought, in clear sight but out of reach.

Nothing happens without reason in the eyes of the Lord. As the sheep who cannot enter the garden but by the gate who is our Savior, it does not surprise me that the only place that we could find to rest our feet and enjoy a meal was at the doorway to a House of God.

>The garden gate is where He awaits
>To open and let us pass through
>One cannot come in, so He bought us our sin
>For our Savior's compassion is true.

In life it is hard to imagine the wonderful eternal life that awaits us. We are surrounded by but a sampling of His wondrous works when we enjoy the beauty that is all around us. But now that we have experienced a brief moment of the disappointment of being behind a locked gate, the Lord has shown us the way, and I know that we may someday pass by . . . through the grace of our Savior.

April 23, 2002

To Thine Own Self Be True

There is a maturity that comes with "honesty" that can never be denied. Your grandfather, my father, always reminded us: "to thine own self be true." One can lie to others, but one can never lie to one's self. It is impossible, and your heart will always know.

Confidence is actually increased when one is mature enough to acknowledge one's own mistakes, or errors. When one can laugh at one's self then one knows of their own self worth.

The weakest men cannot admit to others their own shortcomings or lies. *It is as if a man did flee from a lion, and a bear met him; or went into the house, and leaned his hand on the wall, and a serpent bit him.* But a proud man can survive the trivial mistakes of others, and is strengthened by the acknowledgement of his own.

We are not perfect, nor were we ever intended to be such, for that honor rests with One, and One alone. **Seek him** *that maketh the seven stars of Orion*, knows of every star in the Universe, and their brightness will not a judgment make. He makes us to shine, so that others may see.

The light that we shed to Him cannot be hidden nor concealed. And once we welcomed Him into our heart, the truth cannot be denied.

April 29, 2002

The Good Morning

What makes for a good morning? Is it the soft sound of rain on the leaves on a Saturday when you can lie in bed knowing that you can arise... whenever? Or could it be when you've put in a bad night, but the brilliant colors of a spectacular sunrise put it all behind you. Perhaps it's when your child gets up on their own, and without fuss or fighting prepares them self for the day ahead. Your spouse has made the coffee and left you a note with a reminder of where they'll be that day, and thanks you for all your love.

"Arise whenever... put it all behind you... prepares themselves... and a note with a reminder of where they'll be."

In trying to determine what makes for "a good morning" for me, these phrases seemed to hold a deeper meaning. The discovery of the blessings of our Lord, through Jesus Christ is like the awakening on a good morning. With faithful blessings, a true believer in the resurrection takes comfort and fears not death for they *will arise whenever* into the eternal grace of God.

The sins and the worries that we share here on earth will, through the holy sacrament of the baptism, *all be put behind us* when we enter the kingdom of God. For through Christ Jesus, *we have prepared ourselves*.

Through the Bible and the books therein, the disciples have *taken notes and given us a reminder of where we'll be.*

I should make note of one more phrase from my list of what makes for a good morning... *and thanks you for all your love.* If we chose to accept "the good morning," we must give thanks. The gift of the present must be acknowledged for what it is.

To enjoy life we must fear not death. For there is another "mourning," and it too is good. For the good mourning means that one has led a good life with others. Like our Savior, they have touched the lives of others, who will miss them frequently, but will rest assured until they are reunited in heaven.

Blessed be the good mornings found in Jesus Christ. Amen.

May 13, 2002

The Golden Spirit Miracle

The simple Golden Spirit is not one of wealth or drive
It's the comfort and the knowledge that one must find inside

For the harmony and the heartache are elusive at their best
Find your spirit in the beauty of one's faithful righteousness

When rising in the morning before your day is set
Take the time to welcome Jesus as if you had just met

For in His words and parables there is wisdom to be gained
Find the golden spirit miracle in the blessing of His name

May 21, 2002

Memorial Day

What is a memorial but a memory for all time.
The simple dedication of a plaque in space and time
To commemorate their bravery and the lives that thy had lead
We remember fallen comrades with the words that must be said

We will miss you on this holiday, and every day we see
The honor of your sacrifice so that others might be free
The valor and the glory that we celebrate this day
Cannot match the call to victory; when you gave your life away.

Memorial Day
May 27, 2002

The Messenger of the Covenant

Why do we seek Thee in matters of our own choosing? Thou have prepared for us the way, and through Him may we be received.

The arrival of the messenger of the covenant was foretold by the prophets of the Old Testament, yet whose heart was prepared to receive Him?

Who He would be (**"the spirit of grace and of supplications"**) and *what* would happen (**"and they shall look upon me whom they have pierced, and they shall mourn for him"** Zechariah 12:10).

When would He be here... **"Seventy weeks are determined upon thy people and upon thy holy city, to finish the transgression, and to make an end of sins..."** Daniel 10:24 continuing as to *why*, with **"... and to bring in righteousness, and to seal up the vision and prophesy and to anoint the most Holy."**

The majesty of His presence, for all to welcome and enjoy, was also foretold as to *Where* He would be (**"and his feet shall stand in that day on the mount of Olives"** Zechariah 14:4)

How we would receive Him was foretold in **Malachi 3:1 "and ye shall delight in him"**

Why He would serve us was foretold in **Zechariah 14:4: "In that day there will be a fountain opened to the house of David and to the inhabitants of Jerusalem for sin and uncleanliness."**

These are the questions answered in the days before Christ, through the Prophets. Today we can reflect on them for the truth that they foretold.

In St. Matthew, chapter 3 verses 1 and 2 we find John the Baptist, *"Preaching in the wilderness of Judea."* John foretold, saying: *"Repent ye: for the kingdom of heaven is at hand."* When approached by the Pharisees and Sadducees, in verse 11 we discover that John would even baptize them with water unto repentance, but warned **"of one mightier than me, who would baptize them with the Holy Ghost and *with* fire."**

As you can see there were many messengers of the covenant before Jesus arrived and before he chose His disciples. Later in St. Matthew, Jesus assembles these disciples to travel and learn from Him before His departure.

So must we. We must be messengers of the covenant. Once we have been baptized with the Holy Spirit, so must we be unafraid to face the Pharisees and Sadducees, in our quest to live a righteous life. We must be prepared to preach in the wilderness ... acknowledge the One who is greater than all of us. And delight in Him.

Amen

June 7, 2002

Suffice for the Day

How often do we pray for what we want and how seldom do we pray for what we need? Is the air that fills our lungs and the gravity that binds us to this earth the result of earnest prayers to our Father?

When an important test is to be faced, do we pray for a good grade when we should gives thanks for the fact that we have the opportunity to be taught.

How frivolous our prayers must sound to the refugees who face daily concerns for food and shelter. To the captive of body and soul, can another's prayer for a new car possibly sound warranted?

Beware the pitfalls of "indignation" when a nation of people so fortunate they feel compelled to pray for such luxuries over basic needs; when thanksgiving becomes a once a year holiday instead of a blessing for one's own daily bread.

The wealth that we garner by so few must never replace the compassion that we owe to others less fortunate. For just as we are merely stewards for those who follow, none will last; but for our prayers which shall be heard in heaven.

June 8, 2002

A Blessing in His Sight

The new day is upon us.
A storm is passing through.
What once was proud sits quietly
As melts the morning's dew

The birds in song awaken
With the beacon of His light
Stretch feather, wing and vision
Before they're taking flight

The mission of the morning
Be it fun or daily chore
In heartfelt prayer and praise
Give your thanks unto our Lord.

For when the evening sun rests quietly
O'er all the seas and lands
Find the peace within thy heart
And a pride within thy hands

For although the day is done
And you've done all that you might
In your prayers you've done your best
And are a blessing in His sight.

June 13, 2002

The Burden of My Yoke

The right tool in most any effort can be a blessing, when trusted and put to proper use. The burdens in the times of Christ's miracles were, for the most part, those of physical labors and the survival of the fittest. To make a living, one required manual labor skills and dexterity, this is why simple tools like the yoke were created.

Balanced across one's broad shoulders, the yoke carried around one's neck could support baskets, water buckets or the harvest sheaves of wheat. To some, the yoke is seen as a symbol of "a beast of burden," to others, the yoke was a symbol of strength and purpose.

In Matthew 11, versus 28 through 30, Jesus calls unto us, and says: *"Come unto me, all ye that labour and are heavy laden and I will give you rest. Take my yoke upon you and learn of me; for I am meek and lowly in heart: and ye shall find rest unto your souls. For my yoke is easy and my burden is light."*

For many who were crippled, blind and disfigured, the blessings of work were not to be found. Survival rested in those who were kind enough to share of themselves. Jesus knew this, and acknowledged himself as one *who was meek and lowly in heart. For those who would believe and take his yoke upon them and learn of him,* a miracle occurred. Sight came to the blind, those who were crippled could now walk and others regained the use of their hands.

Just as we seek the right tool when facing a challenge, so must we seek to learn from Christ when our soul seeks rest from our burdens. Only in laying down our yoke, and lifting up that of another, may we, as did Jesus, see the yoke as a symbol of strength and purpose.

May the Lord continue to bless us through the lessons of Christ our Savior, who lightens our burdens and gives rest to our souls.

Amen.

June 15, 2002

Preparing For Thy Seed

In **Matthew 13,** Jesus speaks of many parables in reference to planting seeds. On this Father's Day, the importance of preparation carries a new meaning to me.

Today there is much debate about genetic engineering and the ethics of our scientific pursuits. In an effort to minimize the intrusion of weeds and other parasites that attack our crops, man has developed complex chemicals and compounds. The earlier discoveries of crop rotation, contour plowing and irrigation have served us well in maximizing the output to feed the masses. These are wonderfully successful discoveries, and yet something is missing.

The further we progress in our abilities to maximize output per acre, the less we seem to set aside for farming. The greater the output has yet to resolve the famine and hunger through out the world. Which is why I must ask, how shall we prepare for thy seed?

Perhaps the answer can be found in a parable.

When you hear the mocking bird, can it not imitate the sounds of many others? In the breath of a moment, the mocking bird can recount many songs, and yet, once another responds, and flies unto the mocking bird's territory, he is fiercely driven out. As the number of would-be suitors enters in response, only to be driven away, the mocking bird must expand his repertoire of sounds until it finds itself repeating countless songs to an empty audience. Exhausted and devoid of attracting intruders, the mocking bird moves on in search of a new territory to defend, leaving behind that which it has already secured.

How unlike the mocking bird is man? Ever expanding and in search of new territories to establish, our geo-political societies and scientific pursuits have no boundaries. In third world nations, the basic discoveries of crop rotation, contour plowing and irrigation techniques have yet to resolve famine. Political unrest through the rebellious and terrorist have emulated the mocking bird. Such are those who mock the preparation for peaceful co-existence. They are not unlike *the enemy who came and sowed tares among the wheat.*

For as fear and warring factions have destroyed farms or driven out the peacemakers, fallow ground, unsuitable for habitation, is often all that remains. For as Jesus spoke: *Nay, lest while ye gather up tares, ye also root up the wheat with them.*

In preparing to receive the seed of salvation, I too have *sowed good seed amongst by the wayside, upon stony places and among thorns.* But as a father, I cannot desert the field of my faith for the assaults on my son and family. Even when we erroneously respond to the call of the mocking bird, like my Father before me, I must prepare for the seed, defend the field and accept the harvest that awaits us.

June 16, 2002

The Desires of Man and the Glory of Heaven

To contrast the main events of **Matthew 14,** the desires of man versus the glory of heaven could not be more apparent. While Herod's lust for his brother's wife comes face to face the deceitful test by her sinister mother, Jesus' focus on a holy mission to save thousands in the desert bears quit a dramatic contrast.

While Herod, against his own wishes, has the head of John the Baptist brought on a charger before his court, over dinner, Jesus leads thousands out of the city to the desert, and through the blessing of five loaves of bread and two fishes, feeds all . . . with twelve baskets of fragments remaining.

Consider this, if you will, the dichotomy of the events: one life sacrificed to please another one's earthly pleasures, and one life who is to be sacrificed saving *five thousand men, (beside women and children) with food left over* . . . from just five loaves and two fish!

One in the comfort of earthly power and wealth, portrayed against one in the desert, with but twelve disciples at His side.

Foretelling the future events to unfold, one need only look to these few statements made by Jesus: **"They need not depart, give them ye to eat"** making reference to His statement in the last supper. **"Bring them hither to me"** referring to the symbols of life and sustenance: bread and fish, versus the desires of earthly pleasure: deceit and death (requested by Herod and his brother's wife).

Later in Matthew, Jesus travels to the mountains to pray, while His disciples cross in the midst of a turbulent sea. *"Be of good cheer, it is I: be not afraid"* His words of comfort are offered in response to their fear of death and their vision of a spirit walking upon water. John the Baptist who symbolizes the passing from one life to another through the baptism by water, and Jesus, confirming the passage unto a life everlasting rising above the water.

In doubtful fear, Peter challenges Jesus that if it be thou, to bid him come. Jesus, in one word of confirmation replies *"Come."* When Peter later begins to sink, Jesus outstretches His hand and catches him saying *"O thou of little faith, wherefore didst thou doubt."*

Who would know amongst the disciples, that such events would again unfold in the last supper and when Jesus returned after the crucifixion?

With the desires of man and the glory of heaven, faith is what drives one when faced with the challenges of life here on earth. When the demands of others seem out of sync with what you believe to be right, place not the desires of man above the glory of heaven. And the glory of heaven will be found in your heart.

June 18, 2002

Tarry Not

Tarry not with me, but pray.
The Lord our Savior comes today.
With outstretched hands, He gains our trust
Our broken souls, now turned to dust.

In times of peril, He took our hand
Against all evil, We took a stand.
Not with remorse, We faced the trial
He beckoned us, but with His smile.

Our Savior's here, the way is clear
And by His grace, We will not fear
What man hath wrought, "His will" be done
Our welcomed fate, rests with His Son.

There's a bravery of the highest caliber,
when one must face their fate.
No where to turn but forge ahead,
unto heaven's golden gate.

June 30, 2002

The Potter's Field

The field of blood where strangers lay
Is where eternal life and peace is
Betrayed by one His life was trade
And bought with thirty silver pieces

On Temple Mount they gathered near
To hear the word that He would say
In solemn prayers He brought us here
The garden of Gethsemane

What say by this, betrayed by kiss
Our Savior's life was ended
What value thee, from what you see
Your life forever mended.

July 2, 2002

Unto this day a potter's grave
Matthew 27

The Fireworks of Freedom

What can one say of the fireworks of Freedom,
with the power of force at one's hand
Bursting lights and loud thunder, with compassion asunder
As a spirit casts over the land

Gunpowder was invented long before guns, which is an important fact to remember. Like so many other wonders of nature that have been left for man's discovery, the many uses that we apply to each new invention is as wide and varied as the emotions of men throughout all time.

Consider if you will the many directions pursued by man with gunpowder. Early rockets sent Chinese fireworks to the emperor's and common man's shared delight. That same compound explodes rock for erecting walls and building roads is the same as that which can keep people apart, as well as, that which can bring people together.

When used to launch projectiles, the same bullet that can bring down an attacking grizzly, can also bring food home to a starving frontier family. It can take a life, or save a life.

How man chooses to use the power given him is the source of many self-proclaimed successes and an equal number of dismal failures.

This July Fourth has a greater meaning for all Americans. Throughout the world terrorists have threatened peace with explosive bombs, guns and rhetoric. As our nation's technological acumen has advanced far beyond the basic weapons of third world countries, our own sources of power were brought to bear against us one clear morning in September. Without a single known explosive weapon of guns or dynamite, our very own planes, fully loaded with fuel to travel afar, were turned against us on four separate and distinct incidents.

Freedom is a delicate balance of power. With the power of freedom comes the burden of responsibility. Decisions should weigh heavy on the soul who has "freedom of choice." And yet, with each wise decision one can become more complacent as a sense of personal security grows and one's failures become less frequent. That is when the power of true evil takes root.

We are a nation at war with those who threaten the very boundaries of our peaceful coexistence. When the ethical balance of power goes unchecked or unchallenged, as evidenced by recent corporate scandals, a price is paid . . . be it physical, philosophical or financial.

When threatened with the removal of one's "freedom of choice," Americans speak in volumes. Our nation's spirit expressed by revolutionary colonialists, equal rights supporters and suffragettes laid the foundation of the American spirit. A spirit that challenged one's captures in a POW camp in Vietnam, where a severely battened American gazed threw swollen bloody eyes to re-sew a replacement US flag that was the cause of his thrashing. To the Special Forces who fought against countless rebels to save downed airmen in Mogadishu; and to a young father coordinating an assault on the terrorist in control of a suicide flight, bound toward the White House.

In each and every incident, the "freedom of choice" prevailed over the power to contain or control Americans. The very fate within one's hands could not be controlled by others. The outcome can never be clearer, than when the "Spirit of '76" prevails.

Look to the painting and you will see more than a tattered flag, exhausted and fallen soldiers or a smoke filled sky. Look to their faces of full of determination, the wave of a fallen supporter, and the bandaged hand drumming. Drumming out a cadence to move forward, in spite of all odds; and if you look closely, you can imagine hearing them crying out: "Let's roll."

Such is the spirit on this day of celebration . . . on this **Fourth of July, 2002**

A Plan for Peace

The reconciliation of pain is not an individual effort. As our Savior, and many others before Him have demonstrated to us in their actions, the reconciliation of pain is a "shared experience." Shared not only between the leaders of great warring nations, or the patriarch (or matriarch) in a family squabble; but by the aggrieved, and someone else who will reach out with a compassionate heart.

This morning I awoke, and remembering the death of a small child who was caught in the crossfire, realized that the only way to bring peace to the Middle East will be on a one-by-one basis. To give a prayer of forgiveness at the site of this child's grave will require the cooperation of many from both Palestinian and Israeli forces.

But as our Savior, who was approached by a man with a withered hand sought the help of Jesus on the Sabbath, all of the priests and politicians stood and waited to see if Jesus would break the Sabbath. **St. Mark 3:3** reads: *And He saith unto the man which had the withered hand "Stand Forth."*

Are we all not but men with a withered hand? For as surely as we have one free, good hand to reach out and help others in need, do we not but also have a withered hand that has not moved when the opportunity to help has presented itself? In the next verse, Jesus asks of those who watch and wait: "Is it not lawful to do good on the Sabbath days, or to do evil? To save life or to kill"; but they held their peace.

In the next verse it is written: "And when he had looked round about on them with anger, being grieved for the hardness of their hearts..." Even during one of the few moments that it is written that Jesus felt anger, his compassion could not be withheld, for both parties, the one with the withered hand and those who failed to answer His question.

Today is Sunday, a Sabbath day for me, and my faith. This must become a day of reconciliation. A day to "stand forth" that my withered hand may be healed, and join the works of my one good hand... That I not stand amongst those with a hardened heart. For all that it takes to find peace is to *stand forth* with a heart that is not hardened.

July 7, 2002

The Border of His Garment

Have you ever noticed how one's clothes wear thinnest at the borders, hems and places where they rub or come into contact with other surfaces? The cuffs on my pants fray at the back, closest to the heel of my shoes, leaving a trailing thread. Around my pockets the edges fray, as do the seams, which bear the stress of movement, be it wear or washing.

The collars of my shirts are thread-bear where folded and having rubbed against my neck. Under the stress of hard work, the area around my elbows thin out before any hole will appear. And yet, until the garments are too thin for protection from the elements, we reach for them before venturing out to face a new day.

To touch a garment before buying it is a common practice. Unsure of the quality by sight, to know its worth, it is important to rub it between one's fingers. In the days that our Savior walked the earth curing all sorts of illness and disease, many would clamor near Him with outstretched hands, in hopes of but to touch His garment.

Truth, honesty, faith . . . is this not what they sought? How unlike the masses are we today. A new product debuts, and everyone has to see it. Friends and neighbors talk of a great movie, and everyone flocks to the theaters. A comforting word can be found in a house of worship, and where will you be on the Sabbath?

". . . and besought him that they might touch if it were but the border of his garment: and as many as touched him were made whole."

When you next reach for your clothes before venturing out, be it weathered worn work gear, a radiant evening gown, or but your favorite second hand thrift shop outfit, reflect not on its value or cost in terms wealth or style; but, reflect for a moment of those who sought salvation from but the edge of His robe, and for who the person is within.

That which a few soldiers would later barter for at the base of a cross on Calvary is the same fabric that thousands reached for in earnest desire just days before.

Just as changing style and current fashion compels us to discard yesterday's cherished purchases, what we tend to believe in here on earth today, may be considered but a joke or an embarrassment to others tomorrow.

Just as the cloth is not valued by others as much for the warmth, comfort or protection it affords you; it is more often valued for its style or the statement that it makes "about you."

But when you're feeling down, or chilled, be it from the cold or a close call with a personal challenge, what garment do you reach for in your closet or dresser drawer? That selection is truly important, for no matter what it may look like, be it battered and frayed, you'll care not what others might think. This is what you need at this very moment.

Consider what you reach for in life; but more importantly, why you are reaching for it. Like that treasured corduroy shirt, or soft flannel pajamas, you will reach for it because of how it makes you feel.

The fabric of life is a soft gentle weave ... have faith and you will find true comfort in the One that you reach for.

July 10, 2002

A Wonder to Behold

How clean and crisp the summer air
When thoughts digress with little care
For seldom comes the welcomed rain
Yet cherished dreams will not refrain.

The sounds of peaceful, nature sing
On gentle breeze its comfort brings
The smell of flowers on the mount
Their colors many thy beauty flaunt

Have you ever marveled at the colors and patterns of a flower's petals? From a tight, closed bud, emerge soft petals, with delicate striations of pinks, reds, and yellows or, perhaps blues, violets or other brilliant colors.

No matter how many ways that man comes to attempt a replication of God's creations, I have yet to see truer colors than that found in nature. Perhaps, like digital photography, it has to do with the pallet, as photographic paper enhances a digital image. Or perhaps it is the touch of processor who knows through trial and error how long to leave the film in the tray filled with developing fluid?

But regardless of what materials, techniques or talents are developed by man, the unexplained beauty of natures' colors is incomparable in my eyes.

Perhaps that is where the beauty lies; within my eyes. For as time has taken its toll on my body, and my sight is diminished, the appreciation of the works that we see of our Lord is improving.

For as it written in the book of St. Mark, chapter 9, verse 47, "for it is better for thee to enter into the kingdom of God with one eye, than having two eyes to cast into hell fires," I am prepared to loose but all here on earth if but to behold the Creator of all that I have come to hold most dear.

July 13, 2002

And Followed Jesus "In the Way"

Phrases in the English language can have more than one meaning. Frequently this causes some confusion. In the last verses of St. Mark, chapter 10, Bartimaeus, a blind man cries out for Jesus and is rebuked by the masses. Jesus calls and removes the blindness from his eyes and tells him to **"Go thy way; thy faith hath made thee whole."** And immediately he received his sight and followed Jesus *in the way*.

This short story holds many lessons. First, a blind man who is obviously not well liked by the crowds, the son of Timaeus, cries out, and he is told by many people that *he should hold his peace*. And what does Bartimaeus do? *He cried the more a great deal*.

"In the way" can obviously refer to when an obstacle or person is blocking you and your efforts. A lack of sight was *in the way* of Bartimaeus' seeing Jesus, Bartimaeus was *in the way* of the masses hearing Jesus, for they asked him to be silent. The masses were *in the way of* Jesus hearing Bartimaeus' cries for mercy.

But later, on after Jesus cures Bartimaeus, and commands him to *"Go thy way"* it is written that Bartimaeus received his sight and followed Jesus *in the way*.

Here in the way holds a more positive meaning, for when one chooses to follow "in the way" one has chosen to believe the truth of the gospel.

Today as in centuries past, the phrase, "in the way," is used to describe that which one might not want to express directly. If an unwed mother is with child, it is not uncommon to hear that they are "in the way." Or if someone is dying from an unspeakable illness they can be considered in the way of civic health or community progress, when expressed in terms of financial burden. Although social isolation is a price paid dearly by those afflicted here on earth, to those who isolate, and refrain from helping those who are in the way, a far greater price will be demanded before entering the gates of heaven.

In the next chapter, verse 13, Jesus seeks the bounty of a fig tree afar off. *"He came, if haply he might find any thing thereon. And when he came to it, he found nothing but leaves; for the time of figs was not yet."* How unlike those who are in the way, are others who are not like this fig tree. For as Jesus had to travel to a fig tree that was not in the way of His travels, so too, do many stand afar off so as not to be in the way of those who travel and hunger. In today's world it is easier than ever to watch from afar. Technology has in many ways brought us closer to the troubles that plague mankind around the globe; and yet, in many ways it keeps us out of the way of facing problems head on. We can control the feedback, mute the sound, i.d. the caller, screen the e-mail, forward the calls . . . and distance our hearts.

Share thy bounty with those in need. Be "in the way" for those who seek comfort. Do not distance thyself. For as Jesus said unto the fig tree **"No man eat fruit of thee hereafter for ever."** Be not dry and withered from the roots, but be a welcomed bearer of water to those who thirst. A comforting hand reached out to those afflicted; a yoke to those who burden and a blessing to those who seek peace.

But most of all be not afraid to follow in the way of our Lord.

July 16, 2002

There But for the Grace

There but for the grace of God go I
A gentle hand, a crying eye.
The struggles of a bitter heart
Not knowing grace or how to start

Afflicted with a fear and doubt
Afraid to fail, I will but shout
"Dear Lord please move my soul to live:
That by thy grace so I might give"

My faith in thee, it shall not falter
When I might face thy sacred alter
No thought will I before I speak
The Holy Ghost be what I seek.

When not be left one stone on another
And death betray but brother to brother
Many will come calling in thy name
Not one will be, not one the same

For as the Gospel, be everywhere in sight
The events to come, will show thy might
With nation against nation, Thy Will be done
With the second coming of thy Son.

July 18, 2002

St. Mark: Chapter 13, verses 2, 8, 10, 11, 12

The Word of God unto . . .

15. And he said unto them: "Go ye into all of the world, and preach the gospel unto every creature."

16. "He that believeth and is baptized shall be saved; but he that believeth not shall be dammed."

17. "And these signs shall follow them that believe; in my name shall they cast out devils; they shall speak with new tongues;

18. They shall take up serpents; and if they drink any deadly thing, it shall not hurt them; they shall lay hands on the sick, and they shall recover."

The Word of God unto man I seek
That by His grace that all may speak
Unyielding love beyond all measure
A peaceful heart, that we might treasure.

Though large the stone that blocks the grave
He ventured out, that we be saved
Fear not to enter in with Him
And baptize thee, remove thy sin.

The Book of Mark a journey blessed
"His Will be done," and passed the test
For the greatest deeds are yet to come
By your hands blessed, through this, His Son.

July 21, 2001
After reading of the resurrection of Christ
Book of St. Mark Chapter 16

And His Mother Shall Keep

In my bible, I find it interesting that St. Luke's first two chapters tell of Elizabeth and Mary's bearing child and the birth of Christ. The sequence of the book of Luke coming after the last versus of Mark's recollection of the life and subsequent crucifixion seems to have been misplaced, and we now learn of Jesus' birth. But then again, maybe it is not.

How often today do we learn about the lives of others "after their departure"? Obituaries write of one's most impressive accomplishments and people we knew are remembered so vividly at a funereal service or wake. Why not remember then so with the story of our Savior.

In Luke Chapter 2, even Mary learns of many things about her son that were foretold by shepherds, prophets and Angels. In verse 2, it reads: "But Mary kept all these things, and pondered *them* in her heart." Later in verse 33, when Jesus was brought to Jerusalem for purification according to the laws of Moses, many spoke of the wonders that were yet to come, "And Joseph and Mary marveled at those things that were spoken of him." Simeon blessed them and spoke of how "this child is set for fall and rise again of many in Israel . . . that the thoughts of many hearts shall be revealed."

How unlike all children who are baptized did these events reveal to us the path that is to be followed?

Yesterday we learned of the passing away of one of our former Pastors, Reverend Steve, a wonderful minister who many years ago performed the sacrament of the holy baptismal for our son. My wife and I sorrowed for having not known of his passing, but full of fond memories of a kind-hearted soul, we know that he was a blessing in our family's life. Memories that now seemed to surface from some deep, special part, of our hearts.

Later in the book of Luke, Chapter 2, Jesus is separated from His parents for three days, only to be found in the temple talking with doctors. In the first written text of Jesus' words, and in response to Mary's expression of a parent's understandable concerns, Jesus replies: **"How is it that ye sought me? Wist ye not that I would be about my Father's business?"**

This year, our son graduated from high school, and soon will be leaving us in pursuit of higher learning. I believe that my wife and I share in a sense of great loss. Not unlike what Mary and Joseph must have felt, we know that it is time for our son to do our Father's business.

We will miss Reverend Janssen dearly; but thanks be to God that he, in His own uniquely special way, was there to teach our son. Reverend Hoglund, has been here to continue our son's spiritual journey, and I am confident that our son, Douglass, is ready to increase his wisdom and stature, and is now prepared to do so in favor with God and with man. Last night we spoke with him of the bible that Reverend Steve had given him, and talked about how important it is that he continues his faith in the new environment that awaits him. Like our fond memories his bible will journey with him.

... "and his mother kept all these sayings in her heart."

July 23, 2002

Clarity of Purpose

What is clarity? To the eyes it is proper, unobstructed focus. The heart it is unrequited love. To the mind it may be uncluttered thought, and to the faithful, perhaps it is the comfort of purpose and the confidence of believing.

So much of the Books of Matthew, Mark and Luke are devoted to their travels with our Savior. Having left all worldly pursuits and careers behind them they chose to follow Jesus. What we consider to be miracles abound in story after story, and yet to Jesus, His clarity of purpose can be found so much in the forgiveness of sinners.

To the centurion whose concern over the unworthiness of he to ask that one of his servants might be saved, to the woman who crying eyes washed the feet of our Savior, and dried them with her hair. How did Jesus respond? He marveled. And after healing the centurion's servant from afar, He said unto the people that followed Him: **"I say unto you, I have not found so great a faith, no not in Israel."**

And regarding the women who they called a sinner, Jesus replied, **"Her sins, which are many, are forgiven; for she loved much; but to whom little is forgiven,** *the same* **loveth little."**

It is hard for us to forgive for we have truly loved little. The clarity of the heart is directly related to one's ability to forgive. If you re-read this last word of God from Luke Chapter 7, Verse 47, you will see how Jesus is talking to us all: **but to whom little is forgiven,** *the same* **loveth little."** *The same* is those whom forgive little, and to whom little is forgiven. *The same* who loveth little is *the same* who feels they have not forgave, nor been forgiven.

Clarity of purpose is what Jesus stresses here: "to forgive." It is no small wonder that this, the Book of Luke, Chapter 7, is where Jesus speaks of John the Baptist. **"Among those that are born of women there is not a greater prophet than John the Baptist . . ."** John, who was sent to cleanse us of sins in the sacrament of the baptism, the forgiveness of man, was the same who would preparest a way for He. He who would preparest a way to the forgiveness of God in heaven.

That is the clarity of purpose that we must seek: the forgiveness of many, that we might loveth much.

July 28, 2002

Dreams that Memories Make

What of the dreams that memories make
Of time with friends, for families' sake
With laughter and merriment we join in song
Of days when worries and troubles are gone

These are the memories that bring us peace
When pain and woes for a moment might cease
So bring on the smiles and the joy found within
That in memories made we might cast out the sin.

August 1, 2002

Insight

For unto whomsoever much is given, of him shall be much required: and to whom men have committed much, of him they will ask the more.
Luke 12:48

To be given "insight" and understanding is to be given a great responsibility. Earlier I wrote of wisdom and understanding, today let's consider the merits of insight.

What is insight? Two simple words brought together. Our vision brings the world around us into us for our mind to decipher. The light of the universe around us is captured through our sight. From distant galaxies to the smallest known elements, we have developed tools to expand our understanding, no matter how far, no matter how small.

Of those individuals whose inventions advanced our understanding exponentially, much was given, and yet, because of them and their works, we have asked so much more. How is this possible? Why does this happen? Where do we come from? What will tomorrow bring? To question all that is around us, and yet, how often do we question that which is within us? That requires insight.

Just as wisdom is a kingdom of the wise, insight is a vision from within.

Undistracted from the lights of the world, a blind person's other senses are often acutely sharpened. Their insight is developed from what they hear, and sense in the inflections of a voice, the warmth of a hand, the smell of the air.

Insight can be like a sword, one that is honed and sharpened by our experiences. It can defend us, lead us, and if not respected, it can destroy us. For when generations upon generations chose to ignore their insight, never-ending retaliation in conflicts, as we continue to witness in the Middle East, shall continue... *and to whom men have committed much, of him they will ask the more.*

When man has lost the insight of faith in the Lord and compassion for their fellow man, they have committed themselves not to God, but the sinful world around them. Devoid of insight, they chose to take their own lives. And in response to their taking of other innocent lives, leaders are now pursuing other leaders with little or no concern for those around them. These leaders have been given much in the power they yield, *and of them shall be much required*. I pray that they discover the insight to seek another way before their hour comes before the Lord.

August 2, 2002

The Circles of Faith

Have you ever watched the surface of a lagoon in the early morn. As the sun filters through the southern oaks and the insects hover over the surface, you'll be sure to see a fish strike the surface and as it eludes your view below the surface, a distinctive ring radiates outward, in ever growing circles across the waters.

Soon another strikes, and before you know it, the surface is a collage of circles; transformed into ovals and ellipses as they collide across to distant shores.

How unlike the first words of truth by prophets did their words travel around the world. Appearing in a town square or on the steps to synagogues, by the oasis well, one-by-one the stories resurfaced and are passed from generation to generation.

Last night we enjoyed an evening with good friends that we had met many years ago. Sitting around exchanging stories before our children, it is comforting to know that they will soon be doing the same in years to come. Here, on vacation, both of our families have left our current circle of friends to make new friends, and renew others.

Just as the circle offers no beginning or end, so shall our friendship endure. And although a circle has no defining single point, it holds one point that is common to us all: a center. A point that is equidistant to all who bear witness to that which is at the center of their life.

To all who seek a balance and a purpose in life, it is important to find that which is at the center of your life. For once you find the center, the circle of your life will become apparent. A circle of friends will appear.

Just as the fish who seeks its fulfillment in breaking the surface, sometimes you must break free of the comfort zone that you have built. And the circles of friends that you come to recognize will appear.

August 8, 2002

The First Star of the Evening

This past Friday night, while enjoying a dinner with my family at our favorite vacation restaurant, an interesting event followed a spectacular sunset. The first evening star appeared which I recalled to actually be the planet Venus.

Although the sun had set it's reflection off a distant planet, traveled over the horizon and back to us. Contrasted against a pitch black sky, the reflection off the surface of a rippling tide flickered almost as a signal in Morse code.

How is it that man often fails to see the very reflection of his own sun/son? Just as we assume the light is from a distant star, like our faith in Jesus, we tend to think of Him in the distant past. It is easier to think that His light, like that of a nearby planet, is not here and now. Just as starlight travels millions of years at the speed of light, it is here and now, as is His love.

Just as the first morning star is often a reflection off the planet Venus, we should begin each day with a prayer to the source of our light of life. The Son of man is here. He is now and He wants you to follow in His Father's way.

August 12, 2002

"... and when thou art converted, strengthen thy bretheran."

Throughout the bible our Savior tells us how the first shall be last and the last shall be first; and, the meek shall inherit the earth. Such statements seem so contrary to that which we are taught to succeed in life. And yet, when one's focus is purely on "the here and now," experience seems to confirm as much when valuing success in terms of man-made bounty and wealth.

How far must one go in pursuit of earthly wealth, fame and fortune to find that which we treasure most in life? What cost is forfeited to enjoy the peace found in watching a beautiful sunset? Is the same sunset more spectacular from the ridge of a cliff-side mansion than the canvass shelter of a refugee's tent? When one recognizes that that which is around us has foolishly garnered more value than that which is within us, and that that which is presented before us by God's loving grace is more important than one's perceived station in life ... the clay is then ready for the Master's strong hand to remold.

Conversion is an interesting word. There are many "versions" of life here on earth; many lifestyles, traditions, attitudes and perspectives. But when one adds the prefix "con" a confusing challenge is presented. What is contrary to the many versions of life? When one is converted from one version of life to another, what are they converted to?

That is the conundrum. A person can convert between political beliefs, declared faith, and professional pursuits, but when one is truly converted by God's grace, who are they? How will they know? Can you know who they are?

Knowing of how Satan desires to have us that he might sift us as wheat, in the book of Luke, chapter 22, verse 32, Jesus speaks to Simon and says: "But I have prayed for thee, that thy faith fail not; and when thou art converted, strengthen thy brother."

They who are converted, are everyone whose faith has failed not, by the prayers of our Savior.

This is how one will know that they have been converted, when they care more about who they really are than what they possess. And you will know them by how they strengthen thy brother in times of heroism. Nine minors trapped in a coal mine, almost 300 feet below the countryside of a small Pennsylvania community know of conversion. In the cold, wet mine, huddled together, they all came to cherish the light from within, a light in the pitch-black darkness that shown brightly as to how they must care for each other. Strengthened by their brethren, their faith failed not.

August 16, 2002

Decisions

The decisions that we must make in life cover a full spectrum of importance. Sometimes we give into the pressures of those around us, and other times we are left to our devices. Decisions made at home versus those required at work or in the public forum can often carry various levels of stress or strain.

What time should I require that my son return, to be safe on a Saturday night? Should I focus my efforts on what my employer wants versus what I believe to be more important at this time? Is the public better served by a short term rate increase, in these troubled economic times, for a long term benefit?

In centuries past, many in a scene that played out in Jerusalem required similar difficult decisions. Pontius Pilate and Herod, in response to public pressures, struggled with what should be done to appease the masses, against a personal doubt of their own. How could they have known that the decision to be made would change the world?

Simon, Peter, Judas and the other disciples faced crises of personal conscious when their leader chose to fulfill a higher authority's will; and they had to decide to whether or not to support, deny and yes, even turn on their Savior.

And the people who just hours earlier sang praises of Hosanna, decided to deliver an innocent man to death in exchange for the salvation of a known murder.

In the book of Luke, chapter 23, versus 28 and 31, Jesus speaks of the decisions made and said: **"Daughters of Jerusalem, weep not for me, but weep for yourselves, and for your children."**

For the decisions made that day would affect generations to follow.

And in verse 31: **"For if they do these things in a green tree, what shall be done in a dry?"**

Jesus knew of the struggles of man. He walked among us and prayed with us. He was a "green tree of life" everlasting, in a dry desert of despair for the day. And yet, as the will of God knows what is best for us . . . by the decision to accept the will of His Father, Jesus knew what was required for the salvation of all mankind.

Praise be to our Father, the Son and the Holy Spirit. May the decisions we chose today be made through the compassion and teachings of one who walked among us and knew of the struggles that we would face.

Let us not yield unto the pressures of others who seek to sway our faith, to that which is popular for the moment. But we ask that yea might strengthen our resolve and seek the peace and understanding to be found under a green tree in the desert. Amen

August 19, 2002

A Year of Reflection

As we approach the first anniversary of the September 11th attacks, one must come face to face with how we have responded over the past year. In the year following the attack on Pearl Harbor, the activities of many were focused on conciliation (for those who lost their loved ones), on restoration (of a crippled military force in the Pacific fleet) and on retaliation (against those who attacked us). Perhaps we should consider the same in these days of reflection.

Having volunteered at the St. Paul's Trinity Church at Ground Zero, I can attest to the outpouring of love and support that our nation feels for the victims, friends and co-workers of those who lost their lives. Although I cannot personally attest the conciliation efforts after Peal Harbor, I am confident that our nation's compassion for its fellow citizens is alive and as strong as ever . . . especially in our young children, as evidenced by the warm wishes received at this respite for the weary at Trinity Church.

As for restoration, the patriotic response of the rescue, fire, police, volunteers, construction workers and others at the World Trade Center site, Pentagon and on a field in Western Pennsylvania is a testimony to the heart of the American worker. Diligence for the challenge of the work before them and compassion for the sanctity of the very ground on which they worked, is a testimony to the true spirit of America.

And there is another restoration effort that has taken place: *the restoration of the heart*. By the very spouses and families of those who were taken from us. The stories of their loved-ones, and the strength and courage that they impart to us all have restored the very heart of the American people. For them we are most grateful. In their honor, we must come to terms with who we are, what it means *to be an American*. Devoid of prejudice, filled with compassion, and motivated by the strength of a special love that, though others may envy and assault, cannot be destroyed by such barbaric acts of terrorism.

We should all be proud of how our President, Congress, military leaders and intelligence forces have pursued the Al-Quida network and terrorists that had launched such an inhuman attack against numerous innocent lives and religious faiths. As a nation we are in pursuit of them, wherever they are, and in defense of whomever they seek to terrorize we will be vigilant. President Bush vowed to us that . . . "whether or not they are brought to justice, or justice is brought to them, justice will be done." Regardless of whatever political persuasion or personal opinions we might have of each other or our leaders, there are some things that we must be willing to stand behind if we are to survive as a nation. And this is one of them.

We must always remember these qualities about our country, if we are ever to reconcile on this solemn anniversary. There are many anniversaries of many other tragedies that we have had to face; but as always, we have faced them together. Forever may we honor their memory and *never forget* that for which we stand: one nation, under God, indivisible, with liberty and justice for all.

September 4, 2002

Abideth Not Alone

If one were to relate the parts of the human body with the elements of nature, what would they likely be?

Would the feet be like the wind upon which all that we know is carried around the world? And the eyes like the stars, bright and strong enough to see other stars that are light years away, yet soft enough to sooth the soul of the one before you.

If hands are like the rivers and streams that contour the land and carve out canyons, would not our legs be like the sturdy trees that support all the grandeur of that which converts light unto life? For it is the mind that is like the leaves, which take carbon dioxide and generates oxygen for other living beings, so is our mind that takes in what it may not understand, and creates thoughts for others to consider.

And how does one deliver these thoughts, but through the mouth. That, like the berries on a bush, or the pollen in a flower, delivers a voice that is carried by birds, bees and even the wind to others, to feed upon and digest.

If one were to consider the heart, to me it would be like the seed; the seed, which is the very essence of life. For as everything that grows must begin with a desire, without seeds, little can survive: a desire to love, a need to feel or a yearning to care and to share.

The book of John Chapter 12, verse 24, speaks to us with the words of Christ: *"Verily, verily, I say unto you, Except a corn of wheat fall into the ground and die, it abideth alone: but if it die it bringeth forth much fruit."*

As we approach this solemn day in September, may those be remembered whose lives were a blessing for us. As their stories have been shared and become the sweet fruit that drives us on, so must we see that the seed of their love not abideth alone.

September 5, 2002

See It Through

Speak not my lovely children
With a bitterness in thy heart
Hold back thy words in silence
When you are about to start

Down the road of unbridled vengeance
Is a journey with no end in sight
When one has the time or leisure
To pray or prepare to fight

In earnest self reflection
Look deep within thy soul
To know the will of destiny
And fulfill one's sacred goal

Be it peaceful confrontation
Or a line drawn in the sand
If a war is unavoidable
Make a pledge and then take a stand

That no matter what course is chosen
Nor whatever deed thou do
Seek in prayer to a higher calling
In God's Will you will see it through.

September 6, 2002

As They Loved You

What greater gift that we might seek
Than Christ our Savior's word to keep
That by his hand our lives will bear
A witness to the love we share

No greater love than this we see
That He would give His life for thee
So all would know thy Father's grace
Are welcomed in this holy place

Where evil sought to crush our fate
With actions cruel and endless hate
A special strength, with love they found
An inner peace, on solemn ground

Onward with love, in spite of fear
Hand-in-hand though death was near
They tarried not into the bliss
Greater love hath no man than this

That a man lay down life for his friend
Their death shall bear no bitter end
No greater word's than this be true
Than to love one another, as they loved you.

September 7, 2002
In honor of those who gave their lives to save others on September 11th.

The book of John Chapter 15:12, 13

Not Knowing the Father

There are actions one takes for what they know; and unbeknown to many others there are actions taken for what they did not know. In the 16th Chapter of the book of John, second and third verses, Jesus informs us that *"yea, the time cometh that whosoever killeth you will think that he doeth God service. And these things will they do unto you, because they have not known the Father, nor me."*

Over the past year we as a nation struggle to understand the horror of what we are about to relive on this most solemn anniversary. Many will question how this could have happened; and yet, as we discover in these two lines, Jesus confirms *what they thought*, and *what they did not know*. These two simple lines explain how events such as this, can occur. As Christians we are taught and, by His grace, have come to know our Father and the love of Christ. We take comfort in what we know, and more importantly that which we feel: compassion and love.

To some these may not be seen as qualities or strengths, for they may see us as being foolish and weak. But I say unto you, that whatever is taken through thought and action, without the benefit of knowing the grace of the Father and the love of the Son, is not a sacrifice, but a fulfillment of that which was foretold.

For in verse 4, Jesus continued *"But these things have I told you, that when the time shall come, ye may remember that I told you of them."*

> Fear not the memory of what we now know
> For they that struck no final blow
> They knew not the Father, nor the Son of grace
> To them shall be no hiding place.

September 9, 2002

A New Wine

There is song in every heart. Sometimes the tune is there but waiting for the right words, and on other occasions, we have words that flow together in silence waiting for the melody that fits the mood.

Such is life, for that which is found prompts us to discover where it must be sung, and how it might be heard.

In the second chapter of the first book of the Acts of the Apostles, the Holy Spirit sets upon the disciples, and suddenly they understand every language that is spoken to them. Dialects, common and uncommon tongues are all clearly understood.

11. Cretes and Arabians, we do hear them in our tongues the wonderful works of God.

12. And they were all amazed, and were in doubt, saying one to another, what meaneth this?

13. Others mocking said, "these men are full of new wine."

Is this not what happens when we discover a new song in our heart? When you first fall in love, others notice a difference in your step, the constant smile on your face. Intoxicated with happiness, others wonder what has become of you. Just as the others wondered of the Apostles, you might be accused of drinking a new wine.

In The Apostles' Creed, "the communion of Saints, forgiveness sins, and the resurrection of life" bear witness to the fact that a covenant is born between us, and our Savior. Just as they understood all language, what they heard of were "the wonderful works of God." The communion had begun. The blood, which we drink here in this Holy Communion, is the new wine. It is not symbolic, but it actually is a cleansing spirit. Your body needs fluids, and just as the fruit of the vine draws strength from the earth, the blood of Christ brings life to the soul. A resurrection of life is what we acknowledge together today. We become one with the body of Christ, and as the Apostles discovered, with one understanding.

September 18, 2002

An Even Tide

In chapter 4 of the Acts of the Apostles, it is written that after healing a crippled man and as many as five thousand, the Apostles were brought before the high priests.

Earlier in this chapter it mentions how they had cured many through the laying on of hands, they put them in hold unto the next day, for it was now even tide. Even tide is a unique term here, for just an ocean has a low and a high tide, an even-tide describes a level plain. No longer crippled, nor elevated to a higher station, those who were healed were given a new chance at life.

Later on, in verses 10 and 11, Peter reminds the high priests of how just like Jesus "whom ye crucified, whom God raised from the dead, even by him doth this man stand before you whole." Here Peter describes how society tends to discard the lives of the week, feeble or crippled. Peter presses on to say: "This is the stone which was set at naught of you builders, which is become the head of the corner."

How unworthy are we, but not for the hand of the greatest builder could we become a part of a greater house. Jesus lifts our souls from the discarded rubble of unworthy stones, and through our trust and faithful belief in the resurrection are prepared for the head stone.

When you are feeling low, unwanted and discarded by the fall and rising tides of a turbulent life, remember that the very pinnacle of the church of Christ was chosen from the discarded rubble. Then will you discover the calm of an even tide within; within Christ Jesus, our Lord and Savior.

September 19, 2002

Unbridled Loyalty

The training of a stallion is not a science, but an art. To convince a creature of unrestrained passion to resist its instincts of nature, there must be some give and take. A trust and confidence in both trainer and horse must come to terms.

Such is the discovery of salvation, through Jesus Christ. But unlike the wild horse, whose instincts are toward the elements of nature, we have been corralled by the trappings of man; and yes, even Satan. Believing that we were the civilized world, and the Native American Indian, or Eskimo or Hawaiian to be the wild stallion, early settlers sought to break the spirit of nature.

By contrast, Jesus, in His days sought to save the spirit and deliver the soul unto unbridled love and everlasting peace. What a trainer might see as submission to authority, Jesus sought a greater resource, commitment to a loving Father. Not submission, but salvation. A broken spirit follows for reasons of fear or consequences; you and I, as lifted spirits, follow out of love and devotion to the word of God.

Last week I came upon a golden retriever outside a coffee shop in Princeton. With its face intently focused on the bay window before it, he watched guardedly at his master, a mother, and her lovely baby girl who was held upright in the window. With each new customer, he made a quick evaluation of those who entered or past by the child. On guard with a leash that was unsecured at one end, he stood guard over those he loved.

Now I was raised among all breeds of dogs, and through observing them at our country kennels, one comes to understand the nature of various breeds and individual dogs. When a pet has been trained properly, their love, loyalty and affection is almost unmatched. Not unlike that between us and our Savior who may seem at times obscured from our vision, He watches over us always. The difference in this analogy is that He is the master; the one who taught us that to lead, the one who we must, be prepared to follow.

Faith is like an unbridled leash. That which connects with our Master, but a restraint that cannot be tied, for it too is unfettered, so that we may chose to follow our master, and are free to lead others. Not with force and never through dominance, but always with love and compassion.

September 20, 2002

A Chariot of Faith

How often in one's life do we experience the "close call"? In the fraction of a second, or the blink of an eye, the near miss of death or disaster happens to miss us, by ever so narrow a margin of space or time.

This is especially true in such a fast paced society, as we live in today. Consider if you will, the weight, speed and distance of the automobile as it travels down crowded interstate highways. In the days of the travels of the Apostles, chariots were a means of transportation, especially by the wealthy or those of power. This past weekend my wife and I traveled hundreds of miles to see our son, and I must confess that the interstate highways reminded me somewhat of the chariot races from the movie Ben Hur.

Now, let's travel back to The Acts of one of our disciples, where Philip is directed by the angel of the Lord to travel *toward the south unto the way that goeth down from Jerusalem to Gaza by the desert.*

Here, Philip comes upon an important Ethiopian eunuch who is sitting in his chariot reading Esaias the prophet. *Then the Spirit said unto Philip, Go near, and join thyself to this chariot.*

Now Philip did not know this man, who was obviously of great wealth and power. And in the chapters just prior to this we learned of how our disciples were being prosecuted and imprisoned; however, trusting in the Spirit, Philip even enters into the chariot at the request of he who said he was perplexed by a particular verse. Now whether it was irony or simply a well placed trap to capture Philip, we may never know, but how profound was it that the verse the eunuch struggled with was this: *"He was led as a sheep unto slaughter; and like a lamb, dumb before his shearer, so opened he not his mouth."*

Now these were dangerous times for those who preached the word of the Lord. Just as the lamb unto the shearer, Philip enters into the chariot, a vehicle that could whisk him off in but a moment to certain death for preaching the Word. And to seal one's fate, what does he do? *Philip opened his mouth, and began at the same scripture, and preached unto him of Jesus.*

Here is where one's fate was sealed. Not by death, but by faith.

Knowing that this stranger desperately sought the meaning of the word, Philip rode with him, not to his own death, but to salvation. To the waters edge where they stopped at the eunuch's request; here Philip would baptize in response to the eunuch's reply: *"I believe that Jesus Christ is the Son of God."*

Arising out of the water, the Spirit of the Lord caught away Philip, that the eunuch saw him no more; and he went on his way rejoicing. Was such a "close call" or a "salvation from death?"

Be thankful to the Lord when you return home safely, and to the Angel of the Lord. Remember, that like Philip, you do not travel alone. For once you discover Christ; it is He who will travel with you now and forever, Amen

September 23, 2002
The Acts, Chapter 9, Verses 26-39

Thy Will Be Done

For whence one came, a solemn heart
Prepare thy path from where we start

To glory bound, of faith and hand
That comes before thy grace and land

A sinner's lot Thee sought to save
Deliverance from the depth of grave

The solemn heart of this, thy Son
No greater gift, Thy Will be done

September 26, 2002

What Measure

What measure of a man
is more than his word.
What measure of mankind
is more than the Word.

September 27, 2002

The Appreciation Deficit

In the solemn morning silence
Where there's nary but a sound
Is when the appreciation deficit
Of thy heart by one be found

For the blessings of our memories
And for those we might recall
Knowing thank you's that were lacking
Is a weakness shared by all

For the time we spend together
Is but a present from our Lord
Through a prayer of appreciation
May yea strike but a kind accord.

September 29, 2002

The Prisoner Within

Throughout the book of Acts numerous accounts of the persecution of the apostles are recounted. There in Chapter 16, during the travels of Paul, many scenes are described, where imprisonment can take on many meanings.

Freedom to roam throughout many cities culminates with the imprisonment of Paul for freeing a woman from the evil spirit within her. In verse #6, as a soothsayer, her predictions served well her masters. In verse #7, among the masses that assembled around the apostles, they are content to let her travel with the apostles, as she proclaimed "these men are the servants of the most high God, which shew unto us the way of salvation."

After many days, being grieved, Paul turns, and said to the spirit within her: "I command thee in the name of Jesus Christ to come out of her." Here is where we come to realize who the captive is and who is the captor. For though the spirit is within her, she is the captive.

Later on in this chapter, Paul and the others are persecuted for freeing this damsel of the spirit of divination. Deprived of their method to profit from her soothsaying, they have Paul and the others charged, whipped and thrown in jail.

Here again the theme of imprisonment takes on a new twist. For a great earthquake occurs in the night, and the shackles of all are released, and their cell doors unlock and are mysteriously swung open. Awakened from his sleep the jailer, fearing that all have fled, draws his sword to take his own life. But behold, for Paul cries out loudly, "Do thyself no harm for we are all here."

The imprisoned cares for the life and safety of the imprisioner. Those who are free to go, stay. To administer to the soul of one who is a captive to an oppressive world.

How unlike the damsel and the jailor, are we. Captive to a role that we must play out to earn a livelihood, are we not paid to forecast like the soothsayer; or control the environment around us, like the jailor.

Rising most every day to follow a routine determined by others, sometimes we can relate to the plight of a prisoner. And sometimes it takes an event of earth shattering proportions to rattle us from our office cells, or cubicle confinement. The self imposed shackles of gainful employment give way to the key of freedom found in only in faith.

We all know of such events. They can be quiet and personal in nature, so that no one else knows. Or they can be dramatic and public events of unbelievable proportions that everyone knows. But in any event, they release the bonds that hold. Those that bind you so tight, that your stomach wrenches, or your sleep offers no solace.

Here is where salvation is assured; when you chose to relinquish the role as a soothsayer or jailor. Rather than tell others of what will be, or how they must live, you accept that which is true and come to terms as to how you must live. When you chose to be a prisoner of faith in the Lord, the gates are flung open, and the shackles will fall to the ground. And there, you will find comfort with the prisoner within.

October 2, 2002

For None are the Risen

... but those who art come through thee

When the seasons change there is often a turmoil that comes of the weather, the body and soul. The nor'easter that brings winds and rains from the south into the cold and frigid lows from the north creates a severe storm in the early fall. From the dry, warm days that a record summer heat has amassed, the winds of an approaching winter change the trees into a collage of color.

Hereto, man's outlook changes, from the relaxed mood of soft summer nights, and bright eager mornings, the shorter days focus our efforts to the preparations at hand. Clothes must be unpacked, and others put away, lawns and gardens need their last dressings for winter, and firewood must be collected and split, while furnaces need to be lit.

Such is the body and soul of man prepared for the long winter of death. In the book of Romans, Paul takes us through a complicated linguistical journey; a sort of brain teaser, where a debate rages between life and death, sin and grace, the body and the spirit. An orator of persuasion, the apostle Paul explains law and sin in both spiritual and legal context through the Word.

Chapter 7, verses 6 through 25, is one such passage that, like the turmoil and confusion of a season in transition, Paul walks us through the reasoning. "For without the law, sin was dead" "For I was alive without the law once; but when the commandment came, sin revived and I died."

In every season there is a struggle with the physical elements; be it the droughts of summer, the winds of fall, the cold and ice of winter and the floods of spring. And although life is a struggle for all living things, the sins we bear and strengths we harbor would not be known, if not for the seasons.

Similarly, the spiritual life within Christ and the words of the commandments would unlikely be understood if not by contrast with the sins of the flesh.

Immediately following the law and sin described in Chapter 7, **the efficacy of divine grace** is explained to us through He "... who walked not after the flesh but after the Spirit." (1) Chapter 8 clearly explains the grace behind the sufferings of the flesh. "Therefore, brethren, we are debtors, not to the flesh, to live after the flesh." (12)

If you read the efficacy of divine grace, it will lead you to fear not the changing seasons. That which brings the torments and stresses to daily life will not forsake you from the love of God. "Who shall separate us from the love of Christ? Shall tribulation, or distress, or persecution, or famine, or nakedness, or peril, or sword?" (35) "For thy sake we are killed all the day long; we are accounted as sheep for the slaughter." (36) "Nay in all these things we are more than conquerors through him that loved us." (37) "For I am persuaded, that neither death, nor life, nor angels, nor principalities, nor powers, nor things present, nor things to come." (38) "Nor height, nor depth, nor any other creature shall be able to separate us from the love of God, which is in Christ Jesus our Lord." (39)

October 19, 2002

The Fig and the Folly

Have you ever enjoyed the sweetness of a fig? It is a flavor that is hard to describe. When my wife and I were seeking large planters for a peace garden at our school district's high school, we traveled to many stone and garden centers. With a generous budget, we sought to purchase the most plants, the largest planters and greatest variety to create a garden that many could enjoy.

Once the plants and trees were identified and purchased, with our limited remaining resources we were surprised at how expensive planters could run. Fortunately, one of the last places we looked offered the greatest selection, and the kind owners were willing to discount the cost, upon learning of the purpose our mission.

The most unique planters were discovered in a greenhouse, where there stood a large tree, the likes of which I had never seen. A light gray bark and large, broad leaves were at the center of bustling bees that flew around the tree and at the fruit which had smashed on the stones below.

I asked the owner, what type of tree it was, to which he responded by reaching up and bringing forth two strange fruits for my wife and I to eat. Having never seen a fresh fig up close, I wasn't sure if it should be pealed, cut or prepared first, but the stone center owner smiled and said to just bite into it and enjoy its natural flavor. What a surprise. Although I could recall the flavors of a childhood favorite cookie, Fig Newtons, this was a moist, refreshing sensation. I could just imagine how travelers in the Middle Eastern deserts cherished such a welcomed flavor, especially at an oasis or street market stand.

A journey is often a joy when you venture off your usual routine. The discovery of new experiences can best be enjoyed when you travel through life with the ones you love. To place yourself in confusing situations enhances your wisdom. As explained in the first book of Corinthians.

Continuing on, in both our reading of the gospel, and our efforts at the school, the purpose of transforming the courtyard, which had become an eyesore of weeds, trash and broken light fixtures, was to help bring about a pride that was waning. Perplexed by why such a small group of students, teachers and parents would undertake such a major investment of time and resources, Corinthians speaks to us in how the glory of God works: "But God hath chosen the foolish things of the world to confound the wise; and God hath chosen the weak things of the world to confound the things which are mighty."(27)

Tomorrow when you journey throughout the day, be it daily routine or unchartered territory; seek the wisdom to be discovered in that which confounds you. Dare to taste new fruits, challenge that which is mighty and fear not that which is, or those who may seem, foolish. Because the foolishness of God is wiser than men; and the weakness of God is stronger than men." (25)

Blessed are the faithful who seek the wisdom in the word, strength in the weakness, and answers from that which confounds. For such is to the glory not of the flesh, but to the glory of God.

October 26, 2002

The Praises of Charity

The giving of thanks is like the growth of a tree. Each branch grows in balance with the others and in parallel with the roots beneath the soil.

Have you ever wondered how much water a tree consumes, and how it moves it upwards of 30-50 feet or more? A tree draws water by creating a negative pressure inside which literally sucks the water from deep within the earth. Achieving negative pressures that equal as much as minus 20 atmospheres, a tree can transport as much as 2,000 gallons a day up and out to the furthest leaves. Inch by inch with voids created and refilled, they keep the water moving onward and upward.

It is here, at the thin and tiny leaves that the process begins through photosynthesis and evaporating water. Receiving light and releasing moisture, they demand more and more from the tree beneath it.

How much like the tree is the gift of charity. One half of what we see is "above the surface"; where below the soil the roots fan out like a tree in reverse. If too much grows beneath the surface, a tree can become root bound and die. And if too much is broken or pruned from that which grows above the surface, again the tree may suffer and cease to bear fruit.

In the first book of Corinthians, chapter 13, Paul writes one of the shortest, yet clearly one of the most important verses on the praises of charity.

Frequently the tree is portrayed as a symbol of knowledge, the tree of life, or perhaps, the chronological record as a family tree. In each symbol, I have come to see how survival depends on the charity within our heart.

Just as Paul's praise, verse 2, "And though I have the gift of prophesy, and understand all mysteries, and all knowledge . . . and have not charity, I am nothing." He is quick to point out how we can have wisdom and knowledge, but without charity, we are like the leaf on the tree of knowledge and are no value if we will not share with the branch, the trunk and the roots of the tree.

As a tree of life, Paul continues in verse 3, "And though I bestow all my goods to feed the poor, and though I give my body to be burned, and have not charity, it profiteth me nothing." What value is the fruit of the tree that spoils and rots if not shared with those who hunger? Or the fire's warmth from the burning branches in one's home and hearth . . . to the homeless on a cold winter's eve?

And then there's the family tree. Paul recounts in the next verses of that we know to be true to most every family: "Charity suffereth long, and is kind; charity envieth not; charity vaunteth not itself, is not puffed up."

Paul talks of not behaving unseemly, being easily provoked, thinking not of evil, nor seeking their own. Rejoicing not in iniquity, but rejoicing in truth. The family tree: "Beareth all things; believeth all things, endureth all things."

The tree of knowledge, the tree of life, the family tree are just as the living tree, they all draw from the void created within. They all can strengthen the branches. They all can bear fruit for those who hunger, and a respite for those from the elements. There is comforting warmth to be discovered in knowledge, grown throughout life and nurtured within a family. But they can only survive . . . by the Grace of God, and the charity in one's heart.

November 8, 2002

Whose Will Be Done

When does one know when their work is done? To the artist, would another stoke of the brush mark the passage from a beautiful painting to become a masterpiece? As a parent sends their child off to their first day of school, is there not a concern over whether or not everything was covered? We go over mental check lists, and wonder, did I give them enough money? Do they know which bus to take home? And countless other fears.

Questioning ourselves and others is not a bad thing, especially when it comes from the compassion in one's heart for the welfare of another. Doubt can be a blessing when it gives you that last, important impression; or a curse, when it keeps you from trying just one more time, when success was almost within reach.

I find that "reflection" is a better means of answering the question of whether to press on or to call it a day. To know that Jesus sometimes needed to wander off by himself, to pray, and reflect upon the will of the Father, was not born of doubt or fear, but reflection and faith.

To see a reflection of oneself is to see yourself in a different light. Removed from the feedback of those around you, who welcome the opportunity to voice their opinions, seek a moment of quiet reflection. Just as Jesus wandered off, it was not the end, for His is the masterpiece that continues on through this day; a day when you will have doubts, but will still swing that brush just one more time; a day when you will still send your child out into the world again, uncertain and concerned over having covered all the bases. Now is the time to reflect. Not in judgment, but in faith. Not in doubt, but out of compassion.

And like the crystal clear water that responds with the true reflection of who you are, and what you have done; and, what is the answer, you will find peace in the word of God ... Whose Will Be Done.

Amen

November 10, 2002

The Greatest Power

Power is an interesting phenomenon that can be viewed from many perspectives. Power can serve oneself, others; and, if you believe in authority, power can be transferred or bequeathed to others.

Throughout history, man has found it important to discover one's own power within, thereby taking credit or fault for one's own actions. This false sense of total self control and self destiny has afflicted many people with a illness one might call powertomeitis (pronounced: power-to-me-itis). We are quick to take credit for our accomplishments, and in recognition of how important self-confidence can be, we will even acknowledge others who have helped us achieve our goals. This is not always a bad thing, but when unwilling to show respect or reverence to the Word of God, the results can be catastrophic.

But as much as we think we have accomplished so much, we seldom see how it fits into the big picture: the meaning of life, and our lives.

Perhaps this is when turn to seek answers from a higher authority. and away from ourselves. For to cure the ills of powertomeitis . . . a stiff dose of powertotheecene (pronounced: power-to-thee-seen) is often prescribed. Countless events are described throughout the bible; miracles abound beyond our explanation and understanding. And I am sure that everyone has experienced similar events in their lives.

The Lord works in mysterious ways . . . mysterious to us, that is. If we understood it, we would try to take credit and perhaps we would even try to define the word mysterious as "my steering of us." But because we don't understand, perhaps mysterious is the Lord's way of guiding us. By our own pretentious way of denying the fact that we are not in control, mysterious is a rather ironic word.

Take the time to reflect on that which we think we can understand, and yet know we cannot live without . . . the elements: the water, the air and the sun. As much as we study the elements, and explain them through physics, chemistry and worldwide scientific research, creation confounds even the greatest minds. Theories about the creation of the universe are debated, supposedly debunked and demystified most every year. But to the faithful; and yes, even the scientific mind, "In the beginning" takes on a whole new perspective.

In the glory of God all things are made manifest. And by His hand may we welcome the mysteries that He provides. Let us acknowledge He who steers us, and follow the greatest power to be found in heaven and on earth.

Amen

November 12, 2002

God is True

I must confess that my study of the bible is not a scholarly effort, but one of innocent inquiry and somewhat sophomoric understanding. My own misreading of old English words and phrases often leads to my own confusion and misinterpretation.

The words in the translation of the bible that sometimes baffle me are the uses of words like "y-e-a" and "n-a-y." When pronounced as "yee" the one speaks of **you**; when phrased as "yeh" we read it as **yes**. Similarly, the word "n-a-y" when spoken as "naa'" refers to **no** or **not**; and yet, if said as "ni'" it appears to suggest **no other**, or **neither**.

In the second book of Corinthians, Paul's use of these words are frequent, often together or even repeated; which, unless I am again mistaken, can be read differently, but perhaps with the same purpose.

In verse 17, Paul writes: *"When I therefore was thus minded, did I use lightness? or the things that I purpose, do I purpose according to the flesh, that with me there should be yea yea, or nay nay."* For here, in the questioning of his motives (i.e., purpose), Paul appears to make reference to the dilemma of one's actions being of spiritual enlightenment or earthly gain; the answers to which could be read as "yes yes" and "no no." But if you read it again, and consider the words to read "**you, yes**" and "**neither, not**" Paul could be answering the question with: yes he is using you (or us), and both us and spiritual enlightenment (note the use of a double negative, if read as neither, not).

In the next verse (18), *"But as God is true, our word to you was not yea and nay."* Read this either as "you and no other," or "yes and no" and the point is still made . . . for the apostles' word "is not yes and no, **but as God is true**" . . . their word "is not you and no other, **but that God is true.**"

Continuing on in verse 19, *"For the Son of God, Jesus Christ, who was preached among you by us . . . was not yea* (yes/you) *or nay* (no/neither) *but in Him was yea* (yes/you).

Finally, I come to the what may be the answer . . .

"For all the promises of God in him are yea, and in him A'-men, unto the glory of God by us."

For all the promises of God in him *are "yes" and in him*. And well as, all the promises of God in him *are "you" and in him*. For you see the truth is that you and I cannot be separated from God or the Son of God. That when we do well, the promises of God in Jesus Christ are us and in him, we confirm that there is no way unto the Lord but through him, Jesus Christ.

November 14, 2002

How We are Known

How one is to be known by the Father is probably a far cry from how one is perceived to be known by others. Paul writes of faithful ministries, in II Corinthians, Chapter 6, that we mustn't receive the Grace of God in vain: *"Giving no offense in any thing, that the ministry be not blamed. But in all things, approving ourselves as the ministers of God . . ."*

Approval is an interesting word; for it is something we all seek from each other, and yet are offended if we fail to receive it; especially, when we believe it has been rightfully earned. When broken down, the word approval, or "a—proved—(by)—all" suggests a general consensus of truth and understanding from those who know us. But by what truth do they know us; and, by what measure are we gauged?

Paul answers these questions; with his statement "in all *things*" we must approve ourselves. Continuing on, Paul adds *"in much patience, in afflictions, in necessities, in distress."* After each measure you can almost hear him repeat the phrase "we must approve ourselves as the ministers of God."

Conscience is an important quality to the success of any law-abiding community. In fact without it, little good can result in any society, and failure is most assured. When an individual's vanities over comes one's conscience, there is a void which constant self-gratification can never fill. Possessions replace approval with accolades for what one has, and not for whom one is.

When you read on in the second book of Corinthians, Chapter 6, *the things* which Paul makes reference to are not possessions, as one might come to admire. He speaks not of homes, wealth, food, jewels or artwork. The things that Paul refers to are: imprisonment, tumults, labours and fastings. He mentions pureness, knowledge, long-sufferings, kindness and love unfeigned.

The things that we must approve in ourselves as ministers of God are stated in verse 7: *"by the word of truth, by the power of God, by the armor of righteousness . . ."* For you see, God himself says: *"I will dwell in them, and walk in them; and I will be their God, and they shall be my people."*

Paul knows of the dichotomy of the life of a minister of God. It should sound familiar to us, for how we will be known: *"By honour and dishonour, by evil report and good report; as deceivers, and yet true. As unknown, and yet well known; as dying, and, behold, we live; as chastened, and not killed; As sorrowful, yet always rejoicing; as poor, yet making many rich; as having nothing, and yet possessing all things."* This is how we are known, *in all things*.

November 19, 2002

Survival and The Word of "One God"

Some of today's most popular television programs are what are referred to as "reality" shows. One of the ones that started it was a weekly series called "Survivor." With a group of strangers thrown together in remote, exotic or desolate places, competition for survival, or should we say challenges of cooperation, are rewarded with a greater provision of the comforts of life. Although physical survival is not really at risk here, what with camera crews present, cell phones motor vehicles and helicopters nearby, what is at risk here are one's spiritual beliefs and morals. Pursuit of wealth and fame for the last survivor, but assured television exposure for those who one-by-one are voted out with the symbolic extinguishing of one's flame neither challenges life nor the survival of the most worthy.

Just as in the second book of Corinthians Chapter 4, verse 8, we, the viewers, come to identify with the characters portrayed on these reality shows. *"We are troubled on every side, yet not distressed; we are perplexed, but not in despair. Persecuted, but not forsaken; cast down, but not destroyed."*

For centuries man has found reasons to challenge and control those around them through armed conflict and domination. The insatiable desire to confirm one's presence on earth has often resulted in the death of thousands albeit by malnutrition and starvation, exposure to the elements by homeless refugees, plagues, disease or outright assault. The human body can only endure so much, at the indifference or direct hand of man, but the spiritual body can endure so much more. Just as Paul wrote when imprisonment could not destroy him, we endure much each and every day throughout our lives; rejection, verbal abuse, disappointment and confusion. The obvious answers to our physical needs are far less apparent to our emotional demands. But time and time again, we return in search of a solution.

Living with faith and compassion, in sharp contrast to dying with adversity and conflict, can best be discovered when we look beyond the external differences and seek the internal spirit. *"We, having the same spirit of faith according as it is written. I believe and therefore I have spoken; we also believe, and therefore speak."*

On a worldwide scale, survival is another matter. Terrorism is the ultimate display of inhumanity. Choosing to kill indiscriminately, without need of food, shelter or defendable cause, terrorists seek to destroy "the same spirit of faith." They chose to not speak with love but with fear. Unsupported by the very fundamentals of the religions or causes that they claim to adhere, "they obviously cannot believe." For to believe one speaks with the word of one God. And one God would give no cause for any religious differences worthy of the murder of innocent people.

November 20, 2002

The Image We Leave

The image we leave, comes from that we believe
Be it ever so goodness, or grace.
By the memories we make, that our love not forsake
And forever bring smiles to one's face

Like the fallen tree's leaf, in the rain it will leave
On the sidewalk beneath our wet shoes
In a pattern of brown, that its image goes on
To brighten our day from the blues.

Just as your love and mine, will traverse space and time
Never seeking the darkness within
On the clouds may we fly, till the moment we die
Leave behind earthly problems and sin.

For in faith take my hand, that together we stand
Not behind the lies or the lust
For beside you and I, in our faith will we try
To share honesty, love and our trust.

In this pledge of my heart, that together we start
On the path to a glorious day
In thy eyes I might see, what is special in "we"
And forget not this moment, I pray.

November 23, 2002

Images surround us everywhere. They bombard us through the media, assault us on the highways, and even visit us in our sleep. Though we may close our eyes, the strongest images in our memories can be called upon in a moment of crises or extreme happiness. Like the leaves in the fall, which turn from green to red, orange, yellow and eventually brown, the memories of their beauty can be recalled upon by just seeing their outline on a concrete sidewalk in early winter.

On the pathway of life, we meet many people, touch many hearts and the routes we chose can be regretted or rejoiced. But what lies at the end must be a glorious reflection in the peace of salvation in our commitments. For through us God's will is done.

Bear witness to the pledges that we make, the rewards that we reap, and the thanksgiving we owe. And the image that you leave will ne'er be forgotten.

"Being enriched in everything to all bountifulness, which causes through us thanksgivings unto God."

II CORINTHIANS 9:11

"I do not frustrate the Grace of God . . ."

Do you recall the philosophical discussions of your younger days? When the purpose or meaning of life was explored with friends and teachers back in the sixties and seventies were fraught with mental and physical experimentation; and, a self-reflection that was seldom hid, openly displayed and frequently frustrating.

Both good and not so good results were experienced, as the pursuit of "self expression" took on many faces with religious fervor, political activism, sexual freedoms and drug-induced escapism. When all was said and done, however, how much really changed from a generation that was going to change the world?

Actually, as many arguments that can be made that the world is different, as many can be made that little has changed. We are all products of our genetic make-up and lifetime experiences, but for those who question the meaning of life, as a Christian, I prefer the explanation of Paul, in Galatians 2, verse 20: *"I am crucified with Christ: nevertheless I live; yet not I, but Christ liveth in me: and the life which I now live in the flesh I live by the faith of the Son of God who loved me and gave his life for me."*

We tend to view our lives and our sense of purpose by earthly measures and human laws and values. The search for righteousness should not be sought in terms defined by man, but by the grace of God.

The grace of our Lord has comforted me with the loving care of a family joined in thanksgiving at holiday tables with ample food and blessings.

The Lord has graced me with a life-time partner at my side who has stood fast in faith through troubled times and turmoil.

The grace of the Lord has strengthened my hands at my brother's deathbed, my legs as I walked down prison halls to visit others and my heart at the gravesite of our salvation.

In the courtrooms of justice by man, doubt not what faith can resolve, but by the grace of the Word.

Memories of friends, families, kind strangers and a wonderful childhood bring life to the poems, parables, and writings that make sense when life is explored through the passages of the bible.

In a world of full of confusion and confrontation, the compassion to be found in the grace of the Lord sheds a special light to those who seek Him.

And in the blessings of a new child's eyes, may you find the peaceful respite of creation, by his hand, made flesh, and know that the Christ child resides within you.

For our Lord came down to experience life with you; and, He is no stranger unto you. And by your very life . . . you confirm the grace of God.

December 2, 2002

Sedona

The sand beneath one's feet
Or the rocks above one's head
For the inexperienced climber
Which is the greater one to dread?

Be there winds around the corner
Or the summer sun on high
Press onward in life's journey
With an eye upon the sky

For with faith within one's family
And a trusting in God's grace
Enjoy the wonders of His creations
Found in this special place.

A great trip that I will always cherish in my heart was to a place in Arizona called Sedona. Perhaps not on the scale of the more notable canyons and monolithic rock formations found at the Grand Canyon to the north, or Monument Valley in nearby Utah, Oak Creek Canyon and the many formations with names like Cathedral Rock, Bell Rock and in combination "Snoopy Rock" are sights-to-behold to visitors from the eastern U.S.

The massive jagged red rocks above, and the water-polished surfaces and sands below are a stunning tribute to the ominous power of nature over centuries of time. You get the sense that the earth is being perfected, like a stone under the master's hammer and chisel, to expose the beauty beneath the surface.

With my wife and our ten year old son in hand, we ventured out to climb the heights of Cathedral Rock, where gentle slopes of crumbled rock soon gave way to a steeper incline and smoother surfaces. In awe of the views to be found above the cottonwood trees and desert brush below, we pressed on to the steepest point that we could reach just below the summit. As we sought a gateway to the summit, the wind found around each corner grew more and more fierce. Lacking anything to grasp, and having arrived without ropes or proper climbing gear, we knew that we had reached our highest possible point... well, as far as Cathedral Rock was concerned.

But from this vantage point, what with towering loose rocks overhead, and unstable sand and gravel below, we took in some of the most beautiful vistas one could ever imagine. Shielded from the harsh winds, and scorching sun, Cathedral Rock was a welcomed respite during our first family climb in Sedona.

Further north, in Oak Creek Canyon, a portion of the red stones has weathered to a finely polished surface; know as "slide rock." Here tourists and visitors can partake of one nature's earliest water-park-like rides.

December 2, 2002

Your Christian Faith

How sweet the smile, a mother's face
That's found within a child's embrace
The whispered song into one's ear
Leaves little room for doubt or fear

The gentle hand, a father's touch
With strength abound, and oh so much . . .
Confidence when he is near
A Father's love, a tender tear

There is no greater strength I know
From where ere I be, or where ere I go
A Christian family, a solemn place
The love we witness by His Grace

Though child and parent walk as one
In generations yet to come
The presence of a world so great
Bequeathed by God, devoid of hate.

Walk on my son, fear not the night
In Christian faith, thy will be right
And with thy sister, stand firm and true
Your Christian faith will see you through.

December 4, 2002

What He Wants

What I am, **Is** all you see
What I know, **For** you to live
What I feel, **You** feel with me
What I have, **To** you I give
What I trust, **Love** be with thee.

December 5, 2002

In the first chapter of the Epistle of Paul to the Ephesians, a prayer to the saints speaks of: "**The eyes of your understanding being enlightened (18)** . . . **In whom ye also trusted after that ye heard the word of truth (13)** . . . **that we should be holy and without blame before Him in love** (4). Paul knows that this is what He wants of the apostles, and what He wants them to share with us. "**That we should be to the praise of His glory, who first trusted in Christ.**" (12)

Have you ever stopped to consider what might be worthy of your desire? What process goes on between your heart and your head? Which comes first . . . a thought, or a feeling?

Advertisements intrigue me as I always look to see what it is within me that they try to appeal. These days it is not uncommon to see emotions of patriotism, pride and self-assurances sought by the images, music and words. The goal of provoking our thoughts, however, is becoming less and less important in advertising, if not outright non-existent. I believe that this is commonly referred to as "the dumbing-down" of America.

I mean not to speak despairingly of advertisers for, like them, we all seek to motivate. This is what the apostle Paul does in his opening remarks to the Ephesians. He speaks of their **"chosen us in Him before the foundation of the world"** (4), being given **"the spirit of wisdom and revelation in the knowledge of him"** (19).

But more importantly, Paul acknowledges to them that which we all seek. **"To the praise and glory of his grace, wherein he has made us accepted in the beloved"**(6). Is this not what we often seek in determining our purchases? Praise and glory; be it fashion, automobiles, culinary delights ... are they not also but clothing for warmth, transportation for work, food for good health. What type of advertising is needed to the poor and needy people of the world? Would a refugee care how they might look if pressed to choose between a silk scarf or a flannel shirt? Would a farmer's desire for a two-seater sports car outweigh the need for a tractor and wagon when the crops must be brought to market before they spoil? And what of bottle of fine dinner wine, whose price alone could also feed a family of six for a month or two; how do you market that to one whose family must share a cup of rice and a portion of fish?

Appeal or appease; to reach out, or to satisfy; a need or a desire; health and happiness or praise and glory?

These are not mutually exclusive terms or decisions. For when you discover salvation in the word, you will find the comfort in your giving. For what he wants, is for you to love.

December 5, 2002

Dear Lord

How gentle your words fall upon our hearts. Like the first winter's snow, we know not how much we will receive, and yet, as the individual words, phrases, and stories collect, like the gentle snowflakes, so are we engulfed in the beauty of your understanding and all that surrounds us.

Through the scriptures we journey to a place and time that is so far from the present, yet so near to our daily lives. The travels of the apostles, the trials they faced, and their communion with others, are not unlike that which we face on a regular basis in our lives. Directions must be set, responsibilities must be met and decisions must be made.

But how can we do proper honor to you, our Father? The daily pace quickens from the moment we rise and at the end of the day, we wearily must make our way back to rest for the journey that awaits us, tomorrow.

Let us set aside a few minutes every day. It matters not if it be sunrise, sunset, or noonday break, but it is important that we honor our faith in you, our Lord and Savior.

Just as the changing seasons and the mounting snows of winter require us to break from our routine, so must we seek a time and place to prepare for Thee who awaits us.

And like the blanket of snow which hides the edges, conceals the pathways and refuses to yield the answers until we begin digging, a decision must be made, a direction must be chosen and reflection upon the discovery of what lies beneath the surface must be examined.

Just as your son, Jesus, came to earth to enlighten us with that which is most precious to our lives, let us delve into your Word with the excitement of a child in the first fallen snow. May the impression it makes upon us be like the impression we make upon it. As snow angels, let us spread out our arms and frolic in the blessings of the changing seasons, and the changes within us.

In this we praise your glory, and welcome the days ahead.

Amen.

December 6, 2002

Halos

Have you ever seen a halo? Early masters frequently depicted the saints with a halo above their heads. As if to differentiate them from the others in the painting, the halo seems to float above them, suspended as if hovering, waiting to land, or perhaps caught in a moment of lift-off.

As a child this always amused me. That was until I got older and began to recognize the aura that seems to surround people in moments of sincere concern, happy moments and serious discussion. Sometimes at church, an aura seems to surround the minister during a stirring sermon. On other occasions, an entire group such as bell ringers, the choir or a family at the baptism, all seem to be enveloped in a halo.

Perhaps it is just my weary eyes as they peek through a sunrise or candlelight service. Or maybe it is the early stages of cataracts, or floaters, as my father cautions me that I may be susceptible.

But in any regard, many might think it foolish to believe that we might ever have actually see a saint, by his halo or her aura, but I do know one thing for sure: I have witnessed saintly actions by others. You'll know them too, when you see them. They stand out in the crowd, or are there when you need them most. They think not of the cost, or possible consequences, but forge ahead with a loving smile, a needed hand or comforting voice. Their words may lift your spirit, their arms may lift your burdens, but their heartfelt intentions will be crystal clear, and welcomed without question or regard. Doubts will disappear, worries will melt away, and a hidden strength will come from somewhere deep inside.

No, you'll not know them by their halos. That is for the master painters to decide. But by our Master's skillful hand, they will be there when you need them most, and you'll know them in your heart. And be thankful.

December 7, 2002

Of Those Who Have Come to Greet . . .

Rest calm my weary traveler
Lay your troubles at thy feet
Be mindful of thy blessings
And of those who've come to greet . . .
You with their fondest memories
Of days when we were young
Of whip-or-wills and follies
And glories left unsung.

You've challenged life's great mysteries
And stopped evil in its track.
On distant shores and campaigns
Always promised to come back.

Let not winter rains be frozen, nor the summer sun intense
Be but thankful for our memories
In this loss that we lament.

For every frozen thought shall give way,
to the warmth of this sweet love
And thy memories be they welcomed, as with the peaceful dove.

> For a journey is never over
> When in heaven we next meet
> Say a prayer for those who follow
> And for those who come to greet . . .
>
> Each other with a kindness, for the sorrow that we share
> And the memories that we cherish
> By the faith of God, we care.

December 12, 2002

Greetings

Greetings are a welcomed conclusion to a time when we have been separated from those we know and love. The importance of greetings when you meet, or are introduced to someone new, are very important, and can set the tone for an event, an occasion or a lifetime.

Consider, if you will, the greetings here, today, when we have come to honor the life of a very special individual who has meant so much, to so many lives. When you greet someone on these occasions, you share a unique bond. For as so many have come together to pay their respects, we also gather to fill a void, and repay a debt. The void is the fear that we will never enjoy the pleasure of greeting our beloved here again, on earth in our lifetime. The debt is the feeling that we might never get a chance to tell them how much they've meant to us, or how sorry we are over something said, or left unsaid. This is the sting, and pain.

Just as our Lord and Savior died to release us from the sting of death, we are assured of a greater greeting, yet to come. The promise of resurrection and life everlasting has removed the debt that we owe.

The sorrow that we feel today will be replaced with countless joys when we next meet each other, here on earth, and in Heaven, with those who have gone on before us. A farewell is what we wish each other when it is time to depart. For those of us who continue on without those we love at our side, it is a blessing to know that through the love of God that is what you will do: fare well.

For you have received a wonderful blessing that many in life may never get to know: the communion of friends and family and the sharing of great memories to help fill the void. A reason to smile when a special memory comes to mind, be it a phrase that your loved one said, or a place where you enjoyed being together and with others.

That is what we will share from this day forward, a fond farewell and the comfort of being remembered at our next greeting. A kindness, a bond, a commitment to another greeting that awaits us all; and by the grace of God, we will assuredly meet again.

Amen

When Worlds Collide

How many worlds are in your life? There is, of course, the public world, and that which is aired over television, radio and newspapers that we all share. And of course, your family world: be it a widower or bachelor who cares for their parent(s), mother or father who is raising a family, or student whose classrooms, professors and dorm mates surround them most every day. There is your place of work, leisure and recreation and your world of self-expression. Who you are, what you think and how you want to fit into all the worlds mentioned above.

Like a well-conceived pattern, we attempt to blend these worlds together in peace and harmony and are careful not to let one garner more attention at the expense of another. Priorities in our worlds need to be set each and everyday, else they collide and unravel.

But these do happen sometimes. Some disruptions by circumstances occur beyond our control and at other times by actions of our own making. Your child becomes ill the night before a major presentation at work; your spouse is overcome with the extent of their responsibilities, which seem to go unappreciated; your best friends have to move far away when you have just discovered how important they are to you.

These are the times when worlds collide. The turmoil, disruption, confusion and lack of direction seem to confound you and make little sense.

Like the twister scene of Dorothy in the movie "The Wizard of Oz" in which that which was always firmly planted on the earth, seems to be swirling around you in disarray. Like being in the center of a tornado, you watch it all fly by the window without any ability to stop the mayhem.

If only you could find a place where all is constant and stable. Where no matter what happens in the other world(s) that may be colliding, here it would be calm and here is where you look back and know that all is well in the world.

I've never heard anyone sing the song "Somewhere Over the Rainbow" like Judy Garland. It's like that song was written for her, and her alone. Isn't the place that she describes something we all seek from time to time?

I am not advocating passive behavior or fleeing to a world of escapism, for there are plenty of those to entrap us. Sexual fantasies, alcoholic dependencies, physical abuse or drug addiction are offered at most every turn in every world that we know.

The one world, which does not collide, and really has not ever collided, can be found in one's faith in our Lord and Savior, Jesus Christ. In Him, all things are possible. Not in disarray. Not in turmoil. Not in confusion. But all things are possible.

When you believe in the loving grace of God, in the most important world in your life, in your heart, your faith will see you through. How you feel will make sense, at the moment of crises. How you respond, with love in your heart and faith in the Lord, will be the right action.

And when you pray, your prayer will be answered. Perhaps not at that very moment and maybe you will think that it was never answered. But it will be; and you will understand it when the time is right.

Having faith is the calming moment you seek between worlds such as the threshold that welcomes you as you switch between one world and enter another. The confidence that whatever you will have to face, you and countless others, have survived before; and the comfort of knowing that the Lord is with you and you are not alone.

December 15, 2002

Walk Worthy of God

Delicately strong
Fragile endurance
Expressively quiet
Constant & changed

What may seem like contrary terms of description, portray an accurate depiction of the butterfly.

Delicately Strong
Fragile Endurance

Without a sound, and as light as a feather, the butterfly's wings are capable of flying over oceans and distant seas. Delicate to the touch of man, these same wings are easily crippled, and yet surprisingly strong enough to endure insurmountable odds and challenges.

Expressively Quiet &
Constant & Changed

The transformation of a butterfly follows three stages of development: from pupa, to cocoon to butterfly. Just as a young lady matures from a child to a woman and motherhood, she is changed, and yet constant in her compassion for how she sees others.

Motherhood is so much like a butterfly. With her wings spread for flight, a beauty is beheld beyond all imagination. For you see, she is now ready to fulfill her destiny in fulfilling the promise of life. Pollinating flowers the butterfly is an integral part of God's greatest creations.

Just as motherhood and the holy Virgin Mary came to terms with what must have seemed like a plight that had befallen her. And yet, what emerged, was a beautiful blessing from God, for the ultimate everlasting life.

Just as the butterfly serves God's great plan, when you discover the grace of salvation, you become transformed.

"That you would walk worthy of God, who hath called you unto his kingdom and glory." I Thessalonians 3:12

December 19, 2002

For God so ever loved the world

The greatest story ever told
A Savior came, this was His Son
From this day forth, His Will be done.

What would you sacrifice to save the world? We all have a stake in one thing that is common to us all; and to everything we know... this place we call earth.

How we live, the way we chose to treat each other and the manner in which we respond to events of our time here is all interwoven, like the fabric in a loom. Separate, diverse and individual, the threads enter at one end, and come out the loom on the other almost impossible to discern one from another.

The value of a garment is frequently determined by factors such as the materials used, the number and method of its stitching, or the patterns that appear when it is woven. To compare our planet earth from the other planets, which may be devoid of any life, a similar sense of value becomes apparent.

As beautiful as the galaxies and cosmos are, God "so loved the world." This holiday season, these words keep resonating in my head. And I wonder what it is that I treasure most and what I would be willing to sacrifice for it?

Herein lies the conundrum: If faced with having to sacrifice that which you treasure most to save that which you so love the most, how do you differentiate the one from the other?

God so loved the world that He gave His only son.

What are you sacrificing? What is it that you value most? Perhaps that is what giving gifts is all about during the holidays. Giving of yourself . . . your time, your resources and most of all, your heartfelt compassion to those you love.

For I so love our marriage, our sons and daughters, our parents, our brothers and sisters nieces and nephews, aunts, uncles, cousins and friends, and neighbors and if you continue on your list will grow to include work, hobbies, sports, events, travel, and on and on until you come to realize that, like our father, who art in heaven, you come to realize that you too, so love this world.

With Christ it was the same, and yet, different: for He entered the world as one like so many others, a baby. Granted, his birth occurs under difficult circumstances, but such can be said for many others. What made Jesus different, was that He "experienced the world" and saw the plight of man. And when it came time to decide, Jesus knew what was required, and what it would cost to give the gift of salvation. He gave of himself.

Just like you and I do at this miraculous time of year. We give of ourselves, in honor of this gift from God that keeps on giving. And rejoice. For blessed is the birth of Jesus, the fruit of the womb of the Blessed Virgin Mary.

Merry Christmas!

December 24, 2002

Some Years the Christmas Message

Some years the Christmas message is clearer than others. This was one such year for me.

Not long a ago, at a "thank you" barbeque cook-out hosted by a neighbor of ours, events unfolded that would lead me to understand the true meaning of Christmas, this year. And rejoice for the gift of salvation.

When we discovered that the gas grill was out of fuel on this late Sunday afternoon in early fall, I volunteered the use of our charcoal grill, which was just down the street. As guests had arrived, and it was time to start the cooking, I ran back to retrieve the grill, which, fortunately had wheels. To save time, I lit the grill at our home, and began wheeling it down the street to expedite its warm up.

Two of my neighbors laughed at the sight of me wheeling a smoking grill down the street, to which I replied that my family wanted "take-out" tonight.

Once back at the barbeque, I set up the grill on the back lawn, away from everyone on the deck. As I reached for the handle to open the lid, a beautiful monarch butterfly flew to my hand and fearing that it would get burned, I skewed it away. The person standing next to me laughed at the sight; and, as I reached again, the same butterfly flew into my face and again at my hand toward the grill. Again I scared it away. When I finally reached for the handle, it returned, but being determined to check the grill, I lifted the lid, only to be greeted by a huge ball of flame that leaped up my arms and toward my face. Scorched across my forearms, face and with melted hairs on my forehead, I jumped back avoiding what could have been a very severe injury.

Months later, while shopping for Christmas gifts, I came across a beautiful enameled box with a small brass and crystal butterfly on top. I didn't know why, but this seemed to be "the perfect gift" for my mother. Later, as my family and I were opening our gifts, my wife had received a lovely pin from her mother. It was her grandmother's gold and turquoise pin of a beautiful butterfly.

A coincidence, perhaps; but not until I recalled the events of this past fall, did it occur to me that the blessed birth from the womb, and the salvation of one's rebirth in faith toward God and his special plan for each and everyone of us will present itself in good time.

And may we recognize when His love has interceded in the events of our lives, and know in our hearts that it is for a reason, and His great plan.

December 26, 2002

The Bible on My Pen

The gift of Christmas brought to life
In times of fear and times of strife
"A World as One" we've yet to see
The world as it was meant to be

A gift, the bible on my pen
And journal to write where and when
Oh, move the heart and spirit true
To write it down for me and you

You who brighten others' days
Of when to smile and what to say
A pleasant word, a kind regret
A welcomed day, when we first met

From this day forth, I'll write my thoughts
And lessons from the bible taught
For thanks to you and your sweet gift
May spirits rise, and hearts be lift

December 28, 2002

Forever

Tend to thy mind, and your feet will know where to go.
Tend to thy feet, and your mind will journey afar.

A kind word and a warm smile will open all boundaries. An open mind is a roadmap to understanding.

The young heart in love, may sample many flowers; but, the mature heart with love needs but one nectar.

Build not your own edifices, for His is
                                        The Kingdom
Demand not your own way, for His is
                                        The Power
Test not the will of God, for His reign will be
                                        The Glory
Trust not in this world, for His world lasts
                                        Forever

January 1, 2003

The "-ations" of our Worlds

Inspire—two words: "in" and "spire." To the individual, "in" is that which is within us, "self" or personal. The word "spire" denotes highest point, or pinnacle. Therefore, the word "inspire" understandably refers to the possible heights within one's self. The pinnacle of what one can become.

Inspiration—carrying this idea one step further, when we add the suffix "ation" the concept of nation, or the sharing between others suggests an even higher pinnacle that can be achieved by many who share their goals and *aspirations*: that which can come from many individuals' personal efforts to be, or to do their best.

Believers are those who can bring inspirations to life. To be considered alive, or "be-live," requires action. Much like the "levers" that must be pulled to put a locomotive into movement, believers are the catalyst, or movements, required to bring the inspirations that we share into reality.

Throughout history, this has been true. When one believes in "His story," an understanding follows. When one is inspired by the word, inspirations become greater than the sovereign nations, which seek to control them.

Freedom of thought cannot be controlled or limited by others. Obviously, any effort to do so is contrary to the very concept of inspiration. In fact, attempts to dominate frequently become the very fuel for inspiration.

Perhaps when one tries to enforce their will on another, and suggests that you must "do mine," hatred understandably follows; hence the term: do-min{e}-{h}ate.

I believe that the United States of America was born from inspiration. For generations, attempts to dominate the masses through monarchs, dictators and roaming tyrants ruled the Old World. But when attempts to restrict the levers of forward movement prevailed, and what men and women where allowed to believe was in jeopardy, a New World had to be discovered.

I believe in our founding fathers' concern over the separation of church and state. But that is not at the expense of religion, or ethics, as some would have you think. For churches of all denominations have an important role in the health and welfare of every nation. They confirm the fact that individuals are unique in thought, word and deed.

Here again, if we dissect the word "in-divid-u-al," a "self-divide-of-all" is apparently the confirmation of our freedom of choice. To be whom we aspire to be, knowing that if we aspire together, a great nation will prevail: a freedom to be levers in moving forward by allowing others to believe as individuals.

Finally, I've mentioned another "nation" within this text, without exploring its component parts: "denomination." Unlike domination, where one tries to impose their will on others, de-no-min{e}ation is "of-no-mine-nation," but of "our nation" of similar beliefs.

Although not intending to restrict or unduly influence the United States, or any of our nations, churches and their denominations are a critical element in the success of every nation. Any attempt to restrict freedom of religion, or enforce a specific religion in any government is a formula for failure.

January 4, 2003

Oh Where the Works of Wright

Oh where the works of Wright be found
The glory of design and sound
From vaulted ceilings and wooden eaves
Over babbling brooks, on rocks, through leaves

The windows light, so warm and bright
To cantilevers strength and might
Austere within the heart of town
Timeless beauty to be found.

From Highland Park to Taliesin
And Palmer House in Michigan
Organic forms, red windows framed
Creeks and falling waters tamed.

Frank Lloyd's life may now be past
His glamour in design shall last
As one whose works are works of space
As dwellings with a sense of place

January 6, 2003

According to the Gospel

Unto all good works of men, the doctrine of the gospel is true. Mindful of the trappings of man, corruption, lust, deceit and vulgarities abound in the last days of mankind. Are we there already?

On any given day, the news is filled with the misdealing of men and women from all over the world. Great leaders fall as tyrants continue to reign, unchallenged.

To me, foreign diplomacy must be a challenge, and yet a blessing in a free society. This is especially true in times when in-fighting within our society is in the headlines day-in and day-out. For as tyrants and dictators can suppress the truth in their countries, in an open Democracy, "the truth will out," and for what it is worth, we chose to support a media where what is considered to be "newsworthy" is corruption, failure, tragedy and our own misgivings.

In one regard, this is good, since to be considered "news" it suggests that it is out-of-the-ordinary in our daily lives. If this is true, then we are truly blessed. And yet, with the regular reporting of only the bad news, it is getting harder to see stories of "the good news." That is, until the holidays, when we learn of the good will and deeds of mankind. These are the seasons when all good works of mankind should be portrayed in the news. And so it should be around the world, when people come to celebrate or worship through the gospel that is when the good news must be explored.

Lately, many churches are going through crises of faith for as those who have sought to serve have become servants of their own lusts and ill feelings. Ministers and church members are robbing churches, priests have confessed to defiling youths and Rabbi's have been found guilty of murder. Around the world leaders of the faith have fallen victim to, or condoned acts of terrorism, and outright war.

How long can a world survive when those who are committed to peace under God, act out or preach violence and sin.

In Paul's Epistle to Titus, Chapter I, versus 7-9, it is written:

"For a Bishop must be blameless, as the steward of God; not self-willed, not soon angry, not given to wine, not striker, not given to filthy lucre;

But a lover of hospitality, a lover of good men, sober, just, holy, temperate;

Holding fast the faithful word as hath been taught, that he may be able by sound doctrine both to exhort and convince the gainsayers."

In these directions to Titus, *mine* own son after the common faith, Paul explains the importance of ordaining elders.

Earlier, I asked the question: How long can a world survive when those who are committed to peace under God, act out or preach violence and sin? If we are to believe that what we hear is truly "news" and has not happened before, then the end is closer than one may know. And this is why we must deal with the situations at hand. Look to the Lord for guidance. Pray for forgiveness. Seek out elders worthy of appointment, and teach all according to the gospel.

January 7, 2003

This Day

Where do fond farewells find peace?
A weary heart, a gentle sleep.
To journey's end with your best friend.
A quiet pace. A solemn place.

For whenever time has set our fate,
and welcomed me my pearly gate,
look back a smile when we first met,
and have no need, no more regret.

Though winter's cold may seem so bold,
and sleeping buds will soon unfold,
press forward and miss not the day,
and grieve not for me this day, I pray.

For your heart holds the breath of spring.
A gentle touch that makes birds to sing.
One whose house with faith will show,
the world of love that we both know.

Go gently back in time and find,
that neither space, distance and time,
can take our memories away,
nor the special love we've shared this day.

Amen

January 8, 2003

Fight Your Fears

When wintry winds wail through the night
And dreams that catch a nasty fright
Bear down in faith and fight your fears
Lift up thy head, hold back thy tears.

For what comes of dreams at break of dawn
As sunbeams through trees and on the lawn
They cast your fears back through the night
And welcome you back to the light

Aye, my child take hold my hand
We'll pray to God, the One so grand
For Satan's power will leave this place
When faced our Savior's love and grace

Keep these words, my precious son
When fearful tears, your child will come
For His is the Kingdom, the Power and Glory
The Lord, our God, through Christ, the story.

January 9, 2003

Time

What takes no time to take a rest?
And marches on, be it worst or best
When asked of it, "What becomes of thee?"
The answer found: "but possibilities"

For, no matter how much of it you're leaving
When it's time to go, there is but time for grieving
So grasp it firm, for with it you're blessed
For when your day is done, there is but time for rest.

Time, time, time, what becomes of thee?

January 13, 2003

Hebrews 9—Perfection of Christ's Sacrifice

This morning I read of Hebrews 9, verses 16 & 17, that says: "For where a testament is, there must also of necessity be the death of the testator. For where a testament is of force after men are dead: otherwise it is of no strength at all while the testator liveth."

The promise of eternal inheritance was the question and concern which brought me to my brother's grave on March 8, 1998. After all that we had suffered together, doubt was driving me to what would prove, once and for all, the confirmation of his testimony.

Ten year's earlier, the purpose of the times that we would share, the events that would unfold at my brother's death bed, and the dream that would secure a fond farewell, God would provide an answer to me many years later.

I believe that my brother's death was not without testimony. The force of his testament presented itself long after his death; but was none-the-less a force of strength and will then; and shall be with me, forever.

I believe in "the promise of eternal inheritance." I believe in the testimony of the life of Christ and the power of the resurrection. According to Hebrews 9, verse 28: "So Christ was once offered to bear the sins of many; and unto them that look for him shall he appear *the second time* without sin unto salvation."

The second time appeared unto me with the blessed reading of the opening verses of Matthew 9. Grace be to our Father, and the forgiveness of through His Son.

Amen

January 14, 2003

By thy Hand

Dear Lord,

With the bounty of food set before us
By thy word, may this blessing be heard
Bear we witness to the love you afford us
And our faith to the promises assured

By thy hand, we were formed from the soils
By thy grace we were saved from our fate
While we harvest earth's bounty with our toils
Find we strength to yield thy love and not our hate.

Amen

January 18, 2003

The Second Snowfall

Have you ever marveled at the scene of a tree branch snowfall? After a night of heavy snow, the same winds that whisked away the storm bring a second snow falling. As snow is blown off the tree branches in the sunlight of morning, I lie in my bed and reflect back to my younger days when the joy of a snow day off from school opened a whole new world of possibilities: time to build snow forts, or go sledding down the front yard.

Perhaps I would venture up to my grandparent's house to see what granddad would be working on, now that he was retired.

The second snowfall can be many things to many people. To the work crews who plow the streets, a long evenings' shift makes for an off-schedule sleeping pattern. To the office commuter, rush hour traffic will be twice as slow. And to the mom at home, extra clean-up of snow suites and wet floors will add to the daily chores.

It seems that everyone, except the children on their day off, might not welcome the snow day that is until much later in life when they too get time off.

Retirement might be considered an extended snow day, especially if you've prepared for it. Such is true in life, for as we age, and prepare for retirement, the ultimate snow days await us: for after the roads are cleared, the commute is over, the floors are dried, we too can rest. With our feet up, and our loved ones in our arms before a warm fire. It is here, that the second snowfall need not be feared, but welcomed.

Let the rhododendron leaves curl, as the cold winter winds will twirl, by the moonlit window near, let not my thoughts return to fear.

For a second snow comes from the trees, from whisking winds and swirling breeze. At morning's dawn I am born again, but by my faith and the love you send.

The second snow in time will tell, like retirement, and what man knows well: it is not the work we do for others, but the grace and love we give our brothers.

January 27, 2003

Columbia

A Blessed Mission

You rose on clouds with mission clear
With hearts of gold and family dear
The trials you faced to make it here
The risks you waged devoid of fear

In early morn while we're asleep
You planned your landing, fast and steep
From wings of man to wings of dove
Returning to the one's you love

We rose with eyes of morning clouds
And moved our hearts among the crowds
We watched your star-like entry flare
And cried with pride for those who dared

To honor those of every race
Your crew we watched in outer space
In search of peace for all mankind
A blessed mission that we might find

February 2, 2003

Land of Milk & Honey

What land of milk and honey be
When all around is what I see
A land approved for those now free
His blessings on to you and me

In time may one enjoy this place
Set aside by this, His grace
With ample food and open space
Where n'er a care or worry faced

For the land of milk and honey found
Should all be shared and n'er be bound
Shout loud His Word and make a sound
His glory be, our kingdom crowned

February 15, 2003

Burl Wood

Burl wood: have you ever explored the patterns of a smooth burl wood furniture or vase. Highly treasured for its character and diverse patterns, burl wood is also quit fragile and delicate.

The origin of burl wood comes from the knotted base of trees, where the roots breach the surface, or where damage from another tree's falling might have occurred.

It is here, where one of nature's most treasured creations is born out of stress, injury or the struggle to survive. Perhaps the extent of the beauty to be found is in direct proportion the amount of stress or adverse conditions the tree has had to incur. But in any event, out of the heart of struggle, the soul is apparent.

>Out of the heart of the struggle, the soul is apparent
>*Within the tough outer shell, only time will tell.*
>How your beauty will come from within
>*The twists and the burls like your memories will swirl*
>And the wonders of His works will bear out
>*Once we cut and sand true from your bark we will hew*
>For all to admire.

February 21, 2003

Beyond and Within

Do you ever lie in a bath tub and slide down so your ears are just below the surface? What do you hear? The sound of your own heartbeat and the surging of one's own blood can be heard as it pulsates in a rhythmic soothing sound. Probably not unlike that which a child might hear in the womb, it is a relaxed, soothing sound, to me.

Just a few inches below the surface and the sounds outside become muted and truly background to the sounds of one's own heartbeat.

Isn't this true for much of life? Millions of constantly moving parts, processes, electrical pulses and chemical reactions occurring within our bodies, every day, 24 by 7, just below a thin protective surface, our skin. Much like the phrase that beauty is only skin deep, we spend much attention in life to how we look, and how it makes us feel inside and about ourselves. Entire industries are built around beauty and appearances, almost oblivious to the miracles that are continuing, just below the surface.

In a mass-medium communication society built around images rather than content, we have become somewhat shallow in our thinking and judgment of others. Even the tools of the trade which convey these superficial values are representative of what they preach as "flat screen" TV's and monitors gain popularity.

What a far cry from the days when Jesus walked the earth and shared the good word with others. In gatherings on hillsides and along water's edges, throngs of people assembled, and strained to hear the words of our Savior. Climbing trees and storming rooftops to better hear, and perhaps catch a vision, those whose souls hungered for the beauty to be found within gathered, faithfully.

Today you will find many different images of Christ our Savior. No one can clearly identify his characteristics or appearance ... height, hair, weight, skin tone. No, just as we live in a society where we are told that beauty fades with age, they refer to the beauty that is only skin deep. For that which is found within, and that which Jesus shared with the disciples, who wrote it down for generations to follow, is the beauty that truly lasts: if we look beyond the images and listen to our hearts.

February 26, 2003

Ports of Unity

One of the greatest gifts that you can give someone, is the gift of opportunity. There are many times in the life of any personal relationship that we have a choice to make, and that, in and of itself is our first opportunity; to "initiate" on one's own behalf, or to "wait" for someone else to answer the call. This is so true in every thought we conjure up, every question that is asked and every opportunity that presents itself, or is offered by others.

Throughout the bible there are many opportunities that were faced by those referenced in both the Old and New Testaments. Noah heard the voice of God and answered one of the greatest challenges of all ages: the opportunity to preserve life. Not as he knew it, but one better, as God had intended it to be. Other opportunities that stand out include Moses in his quest to free his people from Egypt, and lead them to the Promised Land; John the Baptist, who had the gift of preparation for the coming of the Lord. And our Savior, Jesus Christ who, when offered the power to rule over all the dominions of earth by Satan, chose the opportunity to suffer on the cross for our sins. He chose the gift of salvation and the glory of our Father.

Without even knowing it, every day that we live, we create another opportunity. Not just for ourselves, but for everyone we meet and know: the opportunity to express the word of God by our thoughts, words, deeds and actions. For you see, we are just like the apostles who traveled by sea; and like them, we must opt for ports of unity.

Where people could gather to exchange food, merchandise and ideas, here in these ports they shared their knowledge of different lands, cultures and values. And if someone was kind enough to offer, or could afford the cost and courage to venture to distant shores, new worlds could be discovered. And a "new you" might be found.

Until the day that we reach our final port, by the grace of God and the love of Jesus Christ we pray.

Amen

March 2, 2003

Eve and Mourn

The roots of many words in the English language can be traced back to Latin, Greek and other languages of old. When one reads the bible, the derivations and symbolic means by which God's words have become entrenched in our daily conversations can be all but forgotten. For instance in the words morning and evening, the last part of each word "ning" is similar to the abbreviations commonly used such as n'er for never, in this case n'ing for nothing. When Adam gave the name Eve to God's creation from his rib, he explained that she was "the mother of al living things" (Genesis 4:20) and "in sorrow thou shall bring forth children" the Lord commanded in Genesis 4:16. And near the end, after God had caste Adam and Eve from the Garden of Eden, Cherubim (angels) and a flaming sword which turned every which way to keep the way of the tree of life was created.

One may ask what this passage has to do with us today. In the evening, when darkness falls upon us, the beginning of all living things is confirmed, for we were formed from nothing by the hand of God, as it is written in Genesis. But out of the darkness we are born and from nothing the pain and sorrow (i.e. mourn) women (out of man) shall bring forth children.

But all is not lost, for our Lord is a compassionate God. And rather that destroy the Tree of Life, our Lord protects it with Cherubim or angels and a flaming sword, now that good and evil have been released from the tree of knowledge.

So it is true today as the vulnerability of our great nation has been exposed by the events of terrorists both domestic and abroad. The tree of life has been challenged and it is up to every Christian and

God fearing man and nation to answer the charge, be it with compassionate love or a determinant call to arms.

We have mourned the loss of our loved ones, and from the pain of their deliverance may we seek our personal destiny from that we hold most dear. Though the terrorists sought to begin the nothingness of death, we hold the tree of life sacred, and pledge ourselves to make it through the pain of loss mourning to the eve or beginning of a new dawn for all mankind, may we pray.

Amen

March 4, 2003

Noah

A higher ground and sturdy vessel
To find within, we must
Above the floods of evil doers
Like Noah, we must trust

In the word that's set before we met
Neither folly nor untrue story
With our faith within we shall not sin
Bringing honor to His glory

March 8, 2003

In the book of Genesis, I came upon a passage concerning the three sons of Noah, Seth, Ham and Japheth.

The son of Ham is Canaan, and as punishment for what his father saw, the verse ends with Canaan becoming the servant of Seth and Japheth.

Now in my bible, a star appears at the end of any verse where it is agreed that a prophetic vision or suggestion of Christ is contained in the verse. So what prophesy was contained herein? For having seen the truth of his father, the son of Ham, Canaan, tells the others what his father saw; and, is destined to spend his days as a servant to those he told.

If we substitute "man" for Ham, "Jesus" for Canaan and "mankind" for those he told... the prophesy of Christ becomes apparent.

For having seen the truth of his father, the son of **Man, Jesus**, tells the others what he knows of the Father; and, is destined to spend his days as a servant to **mankind**. "To tell others what his father had seen" and, at the hands of those he has told, must he suffer.

March 11, 2003
Genesis 10:18-27

A Compassionate Lot

On the eve of the destruction of Sodom we find a compassionate man caught between his family and neighbors in defense of two strangers. Having come to judge Sodom, the two angels were offered refuge in Lot's home. Outside his door masses of Sodomites gathered, demanding that the strangers be delivered unto them. Knowing what fate both Sodom would soon face, if the mobs would not turn away, Lot pleaded with them against their madness. When the mobs sought to charge Lot's door, the Lord blinded them, so they would wander aimlessly (Genesis 19:1-11).

How frequently are we also blinded by rage? When anger swells up inside us and we can't hear reason or see the folly of our ways, do we not also fail to accomplish our misguided goals; or if do not fail, do we not regret our actions when the blindness has lifted?

Lot left Sodom with his wife and two daughters. Instructed "not to look back" Lot's wife turned and became a pillar of salt (Genesis 19:15, 16, 26). When one has no regrets, true appreciation is realized. This is what the Lord seeks from us, for as His Son died on the cross at Calvary, the greatest sacrifice without regrets was proven to be possible.

March 16, 2003

The Watershed

A few years ago I wrote of the spring house at our old farm house near Pittsburgh. As a place of peaceful respite, the collection of precious water and comfort is a place that many seek. But a thought occurred to me is, what is it that brings us to such a place? The watershed in geographical terms could be described as the area where water not only collects, but is directed by forces of gravity to a common stream, river, lake or other body of water. Just as societies are made up of many diverse sources and backgrounds, they serve as the watershed of civilization here on earth. When drawn together by a common bond or force of nature, thoughts, opinions and perspectives collect together. Just as droplets of rain puddle and then grow, soon they gain sufficient mass to more forward toward an unknown goal or common vision that is yet to be realized. As in any geographical watersheds, obstacles and diversions may hinder their progress, blur the path from being straight and narrow, some puddles must wait for others to join them before moving on. Soon with adequate input and substantial backing, the water is shed from the impediments that bar its way to its destined purpose. To bring life to creatures large and small, a source of power to those with imagination, a method of travel to those who long for adventure, and a quiet peaceful place of solitude to those who prepare and reflect on the memories of a springhouse called home.

Today, all over the world, many await an answer to their purpose in life. Some feel that they know the answer, and are compelled to fulfill their role as either an impediment or pathway to the steady progress of mankind. Others assemble in small groups seeking out ideas and alternatives before venturing forward; waiting for others to arrive, or for obstacles to be removed. Drawn together by unseen forces we all eventually travel together, however. Our source and our destination are one and the same. Just as the cycle of life for water here on earth repeats itself by the grace of God, so shall we serve His purpose in the watershed cycle of faith. For we shall be as one rain drop at birth, falling together as families, assembling as friends, developing into neighbors, growing to become cities and swelling into nations. And if we are fortunate, and let not ourselves become deterred from our destined, common purpose, we can flow past the hatred, prejudices, ill-gotten gains and evil diversions, to begin our Father's will: that we live in peace and harmony.

Blessed be the Will of God
And We our Faith within
Rising with the Tide of Love
Resisting Evil's Sin

For Wherever There's Deterrence
Or Obstacles in Our Way
Let the Watershed of Compassion
Assemble in Faith, I Pray.

March 19, 2003

Reminders

Reminders are nature's way of telling us something we may, or are likely to, forget. How one decides what to remember and what to discard can be pretty much a subconscious act. For when we state that we'll just forget that, and put it out of our mind, it usually means that it has obviously made a significant impression; and, is one that we are unlikely to ever forget.

But what in life are reminders? A story that a pastor in a local church recounted to our children was the story of Noah and the great flood. At the end of the story, God creates a rainbow to appear as a reminder of his great love for the world, and all creation. To remind Him of how much He truly loves us, so that His anger may never be so great as to destroy all life, so He promises Noah.

Life everlasting, through Jesus Christ comes much later. The cross has become our reminder to us that God's promise is fulfilled. Just as the Lord required a reminder through the beauty of a rainbow following the end of a storm, our wrath will cease at the foot of the Calvary. It is in the shadow of the cross where we might gaze toward the Son, and not be blinded by the truth.

> Beneath the cross of Calvary
> Is where the truth that I might see
> The blessings of eternity
> A promise kept for you and me.
>
> As our Lord's wrath on all mankind
> Where nary be an earth to find
> On Noah's faith did He Remind?
> His love prevailed on rainbows lined.

With brilliant colors that never end
His promise true that He did send
To heal all ills and sorrows mend
The Word of God, we will defend.

March 24, 2003

The Blessings of the Son

Throughout the bible there are various times when the father's blessings of their children are in direct conflict with the wishes of the sons' or others present. In Genesis, Chapter 48; 13-21, Joseph's two sons join hands with their father and dying grandfather, Jacob, Jacob's eyes are failing, and contrary to the wishes of his son, Jacob's right is placed on the younger child, Ephraim, and not on the first born, Manasseh. In reply to Joseph's displeasure and attempt to reverse the hands of his father, Jacob replies "I know it, my son, I know it. And he shall also become a people, and he shall also be great: but truly his younger brother shall become greater than he, and his seed shall become a multitude of nations."

The importance of this passage is intensely apparent to Joseph, who, if you recall was sold into slavery, and given for dead by his own brothers. For years, Jacob did not know that his presumed dead son, Joseph, had risen to greatness in Egypt, and not until a draught brought his brothers to him for corn, was Joseph forgiving and reunited with his father.

From the very moment of Jacob's birth, as he entered the world on the heals of his twin brother Esau (see Chapter 25) throughout events of the transfer of birthrights for a price and then back again through deceit at their father's deathbed (see Chapter 27), the pursuit of one's father's blessings causes man to act in very strange and often dishonest ways.

How unlike today when the pursuit of our Father's blessing do we lie, deceive, corrupt and take advantage of our position in life, or the favor of another. Pride truly rises before a fall, but regardless of what we pursue, our Father's Will be done, on earth, as it is in heaven.

Amen

April 4, 2003

The Love in One's Land

No soil is foreign
On this God's green earth
For He measures it not
By its value or worth

Treasure we by its beauty
And all that is grand
Although nothing is owned
Save it not by His hand

Preserve and not waste it
Cherish all that is found
For the yield that yea harvest
Not all comes from the ground

Unrest and false pride
Peradventure we reap
But by all that is sacred
It's His love, we must seek

When preparing one's garden
Must one's soil be tilled
By the voice of its people
Unearth passionate willed

For no stranger is foreign
When one takes a hand
With compassion and grace
And the love in one's land.

April 5, 2003

It Is

Two words of truth, can not deny
No matter where or how one try
To find within, just before a lie
"It is" truth to face, before we die

We talk of what we want to say
In hopes that others see our way
"What was" forgotten, is what we pray
To face the truth, adjourn "this day"

The journey life fraught with despair
When lies appear, out of thin air
The deeper hole, the larger the snare
"It is the truth" that one would declare

One would say: "as it is this day"
It is God's Will, from that, what may
Be gathered dust, unto molded clay,
Our lives to save, many people pray.

April 7, 2003

Genesis Chapter 50, verse 20:

"For as for you, ye thought evil against me; *but* God meant it unto good, to bring to pass, as **it is** this day, to save much people alive."

The Bee Line Prayer

The soft white petals seem to glow under the radiant moon above. By evening's call, the large bees' journey from one blossom to another while the short seasonal harvest begins. Time is too short for the weary bee that has but one mission: to serve the hive before summer's heat prevails.

Studies of honey bees are fascinating. In early Spring their search for the source of nectar, winds their flight path in random motions to and fro. Once discovered, however, the bee flies back to the hive. There an intricate dance and motions of the bee are conducted in the darkest recesses of the hive. Somehow, "exact coordinates" to the flowering petals is conveyed, and the other bees fly directly to the flowering petals; hence the term "bee line."

Today, man has created many forms of communication between a diverse and ever changing world of language, geopolitical and cultural boundaries and surface conditions. In the liberation of Iraq, cruise missiles guided by GPS coordinates and optical recognition systems "bee lined" them straight to their intended targets. On the ground infantry units with small, hand held language interpreter computers recite phrases and instructions between American soldiers and the Iraqi people.

Communications that have failed in search of peaceful resolution often triumph in combat or strife where one's very life, if not pride, is at stake. Here is where the lines are drawn between brutal dictatorships and the compassionate liberators of the world.

If tomorrow you awoke, and learned of a direct path that leads to salvation, how would you react? Would you question its credibility, its source and the means in which it was delivered? Or place it at the end of a long to-do list, promising to get to it when you could? Or like the rare few, who embrace the Word, faithfully, and with an open heart, drop everything and go straight to the Source?

Just as with the searching bee, the direction to be taken is seldom a clear line that one can see, be it day or night. And to travel in due time, for the season of man is short, requires not the wings of an angel, but the heart of a believer. Just as the delicate petals of a life here on earth wither, fade and fall, the promise of an everlasting tree in heaven awaits you. There you will find the sweet nectar of love to be found, abundant and eternal.

This Easter, as we scurry around making preparation for His return, close your eyes for a moment; and, in the darkness that surrounds you, pray for a straight and true direction. Toward the salvation to be found with faith in the One who has returned from the darkness of death, Christ Jesus, our risen Lord and Savior.

Amen

April 15, 2003

Traditions

Traditions hold a special place in the hearts of every family and extended sphere of friendships. What we are each expected to do or attempt to do is as much a function of what we and others have done before us and the anticipation of what will result. A common sense of security eventually evolves, as a specific set of norms is once again confirmed.

But what of the rebel, or the nonconformist who is driven by a personal mandate or inner spiritual directive, such individuals' actions have been known to disrupt and dismay others. Such was the case with Elisabeth and Zacharias, parents of the child who would later become the apostle John, "John the Baptist" would all come to understand. In Luke 1: 57-63. Elisabeth declares that their son's name shall be John; and not in accordance with the tradition, Zacharias, according to his father.

A crew team rows up Lake Carnegie. In unison, the oars lift and are pushed forward before returning to the water's surface. Like the goose whose wings lift to take flight, the silhouette of the crew from behind seems to take wing on the water, pressing forward above the waves, only to return and pull against the water.

A single skull glides by under the power of its own strength, or so it seems. Unable, or perhaps unwilling to gain sufficient speed to catch up with the eight man crew, the lone skull is not unlike John the Baptist, who chose to wait for another who would lead. For just as the geese fly in a traditional "V" formation, so has John waited patiently, to welcome the One who would lead in a truer direction and join in the mission.

I watched a gosling, its head fervently dipping below the water to force the cascading waves over its back, and remembered my baptism.

April 22, 2003

The Garden Path

My wife and I love a good garden, and garden path. To walk along a safe route and admire the beautiful flowers, plants, rocks and water features is truly a marvel to behold. To reflect upon the time and effort that one or others must have committed before to create such a pleasant place to journey, is a credit to the gift of industry given by God unto man. But the industrious spirit can be equally dangerous and harmful when one ventures off the path and seeks temptations of self serving interests with no regards for the welfare of others. I once wrote on the variations of the English language suffix: "ations." Here again the world of tempt(ation) suggests a world of sinful desires. But then I noticed the prefix "temp" as in temporary. This is what we must consider when faced with a decision between good versus evil. For good, and godliness are eternal, but temptations are truly temporary.

Dear Lord,
In your image, you have instilled in us a great desire to create, and the qualities of industry, dedication to hard work and a desire to excel. You let us make great strides in our personal lives and professional careers. But sometimes we must ask, to what reward, if not to the glory of you? You, who are the creator of all that we know, and have yet to discover. You who know the answers before the questions are asked and the motivation behind our every thought, deed and effort. Our temptations, our weaknesses, and our ill-conceived plans that lead us off the very path set before us, cannot deter your love and patience to be there when we return. Let us look to the examples set by your Son, in Luke 4 versus 1 through 13, for

here is where Christ Jesus resisted the temptations of Satan. Here is where He spoke the truth for what man truly lives by, who man must serve and why man shall not tempt.

Just as the last verse, 13 reads: "And when the devil had ended all the temptation, he departed from him **for a season**." So shall temptations depart from us, when we chose the right path to follow. And when we stray, may we be thankful that you are there to guide us back, by the grace of Jesus Christ. And until such time that the seasons of temptations may end forever, may all the glory and praise be directed to where it rightly belongs: to God, the Father, the Son and the Holy Spirit.

Amen

April 24, 2003

Through Visions Clear

Who welcomes faith through visions clear
A restless heart, a mission dear
Arising from the burial cave
Into my soul that it be saved

For though He walked among the crowd
Hosanna's ringing strong and loud
He knew what soon they all would see
Upon the cross at Calvary

In huddled groups they sought His robe
Soon to face the trials like Job
What manner of a man was He?
They came to know what they would see:

Salvation from the sting of death
With His last words and final breath
Unto the Father, for "It is done"
The battle over death is won.

We welcome faith through visions clear
The words we listen, and long to hear
His life was like the morning light
Our love and faith, now shining bright.

May 8, 2003

In The Company of Strangers

Throughout the bible Jesus talks with His disciples of traveling to distant places to spread the word of God. Devoid of possessions and adequate funding, they were instructed to seek the hospitality of others, and reside in the company of strangers. In the company of strangers; how often today do we find ourselves seeking the generosity and hospitality of strangers? In a society founded on principles of self-sufficiency, where are you most likely to come across the personal needs of others? Has anyone ever knocked on your door and requested a place to sleep out of the elements? Or when hotels and motels are filled to capacity, would you consider the prospect of approaching a stranger for a place to stay?

We all know of the blessed story of Jesus' birth and the meager manger. Well here in our small high school courtyard, a wood duck has chosen to bear her young through a small nest hidden behind an azalea. Now mind you, there is no way in or out but by two doors, one off the cafeteria and the other off the hall, and the open sky above. Here is where my wife and other volunteers have converted an overlooked, neglected asset into a lovely urban garden. And here is where this duck has chosen to find safety from its natural predators, in the company strangers. Last year, her eggs bore beautiful ducklings, which were then taken to the nearby Colonial Lake. And yet, she has once again returned this year to lay another brood of siblings. Now that they have hatched and moved on, what did we find the other day? But yet another nest of eggs which are probably from a child or another duck that discovered where a safe harbor can be found in the company of strangers.

To many, like the followers of Jesus, strangers are merely friends whom you have yet to meet. And as the disciples were instructed in the book of Luke, they were to shake the dust off their feet upon leaving those where they were not welcomed.

> If one continues to turn away strangers,
> Soon there will be no friends.
> When one accepts the kindness of strangers,
> Christian friendships will know no ends.

May 14, 2003

Pilate & Herod

The Validation Sought

In Luke 23:12 it is interesting to note how Pilate and Herod "were made friends together: for before they were enemies between themselves." Even as Jesus knew that they would not answer him, an innocent man accused, they were willing to put their differences aside knowing that they could use each other for the unjust sentence that the mobs would demand.

Pilate delivered Jesus "to their will" so he had thought. Though the truth be known, it was the will of God that would prevail. Choosing not to answer his interrogators, Jesus replied **"Thou sayest it."** For an innocent man need not reply, and yet to be unjust the accusers each sought a validation, even if at the hands of their enemies.

Where one turns for validation says a lot about a person. The steps that we take to justify our actions, and the confidences we seek are all too often without consultation with our Lord and Savior.

Later on, after the horrific crucifixion of Jesus, He appears and walks with the disciples and recounts the teachings to those who are caught up in their grief and confusion of recent events. Like those of us who return to the foundation of our faith after facing a challenge alone, we rediscover the guidance that was ready to save us from harm or humiliation. The validation was there, had we only sought the word of God.

In the days that lie ahead, I pray that the decisions to be made be guided not by the validation of others, but by the grace and guidance of a loving Father and gentle Son who will always be there when I look into my heart.

Amen

May 30, 2003

Where We Will Find

"Why do you seek the living among the dead?" Some questions are as true today as they were thousands of years ago. We see Christ as the crucified, and not as the risen. For today He is as alive as He was when He walked among the crowds that gathered to hear His words. Just as today, we do the same; with our hearts yearning, our spirits longing and our love enduring. With Jesus, we discover the living Christ within us all.

Amen

May 30, 2003

Dear Lord,

I have prayed to thee with a solemn heart and an undeserved pride born of the sinful trappings of Satan. Quick to judge others, while failing to confess mine own faults and failings, I come to you this morning as a broken vessel of no value to any, but say to discard among the lost and undeserved. With but one hope left, that though I must suffer the persecution of others, I might not succumb but for one salvation and prayer for that which I hold most dear: the love of Christ, your son and but all my only hope, that I might be forgiven.

Dear Lord, let me relinquish all foolish pride of man, that my spirit may be lifted, regardless of the depths of hell that might otherwise be my fate here. For as those whom I know that thou hast saved, may I be counted among the sinners who but reach for thy Son's robe, climb that I might hear His Word, and walk into the depths that I might find the true path of righteousness through the eyes and blessings of my Lord and Saviour, Jesus, I pray.

Amen

June 6, 2003

Saviour (Savior)

The word has a soft, reassuring ring to it. So seldom is it spoken outside of religious circles; and yet, He is the first One that we turn to in moments of dire consequences. In the past, Savior was spelled Saviour. Today it is spelled Savior. Perhaps the following can explain the one spelling; and I'll leave it to the reader as to what the more current version's spelling might mean.

The word, if broken down, is where we find the words Sav(e)-I-Our. The use of singular and plural pronouns, "I" and "our" in sequence intrigues me. Could it suggest "save me our . . . Father who art in heaven"? Or could it refer to save me what is ours: our faith, in spite of "our sins," perhaps.

Save is often used in place of the word "put away" or "set aside." Perhaps in this case, the Savior is the One who is prepared to relinquish one (I) for the many (our). The ultimate sacrifice: for that is what Jesus truly is; and, as our Saviour, what He was willing to do on the cross at Calvary.

> Oh Lord of all you've yet to show
> Our faith within thy Son doeth grow
> Of words we read, and deeds we sow
> A Saviour that our hearts will know

June 12, 2003

Remember Your Baptism

What drifts among the morning's mist
In waters clear and memories crisp
Recall the days when we were young
As blessings of a life redone

For with strong will and faith renewed
We'll find the strength to see it through
What years are left be no regrets
One path is true, the course is set

Like the one in wilderness alone
Cry loud your sins, we must atone
From heaven's form, alight like a dove
Upon the Son, the One is love

June 11, 2003
Luke 3 verses 4 & 22

All Honor, Praise and Glory

"**Surely men of low degree are of vanity and men of high degree are a lie:** . . ." Recognition is sometimes misunderstood, for those who seek it, seek it either of themselves or of others. When one's self confidence is overwhelming, vanity or egotism abounds. And when another is placed above all others in stature or through accolades beyond reproach, it is hard to consider that they are not so different than you, I or anyone else.

This is the dilemma of those who seek to excel in some pursuit, or others who garner unimaginable attention or recognition.

Psalm 62, verse 9, forewarns us of such trappings. And the humble spirit must face this truth every time that they feel good about themselves, be it self satisfaction or the praise of others. The same holds true for those who accept defeat and are of low self-esteem.

But verse 9 continues: "**. . . to be laid in the balance, they are altogether *lighter* than vanity.**" The truth is whether or not of low or high degree, vanity outweighs all. Men who justify their own failings, shortcomings or resentment of others hide behind the same vanity as also the lie of those who think too highly of themselves, or are placed upon a pedestal by others. "Placed altogether" seems to suggest that even of those who seem genuinely destitute or downtrodden or others who are highly esteemed, wonderful people, we should recognize that our own efforts to assist the one or praise the other can become actions that weigh in on the scale on the side of vanity.

Similarly, for those who are genuinely destitute or downtrodden, free will and the word of God offer a means and direction for self-help if they so desire to not be a burden to others. To the highly praised individual, the truth of humility before God and the recognition of the responsibility placed on them by others requires a similar special strength of character.

Vanity will lead us to live a life of lies. For the truth be told, **for unto thee, O Lord belongeth mercy: for thou renderest to every man according to his work**. And we must remind ourselves constantly of the plight that we suffer or success that we enjoy, and consider why God has allowed one or placed the other upon us: for although we do not know how the Lord works in such mysterious ways, we do need to explore our own actions and motivations. With an honest evaluation, and seek help from others and the written word. And remember, that all Honor, Praise and Glory be unto our Father, who art in heaven.

Amen

June 15, 2003

A Warrior's Lament

From where one walks on distant shores
In days of love and legend's lores
Bring back what tales and peradventure
Seek glory bound and moments tender

Round fires of warriors' nights' encampment
With words of home and their enchantment
Sing songs of woe and lonely days
More fierce and hotter than the blaze

Rage strong within our hearts' lament
With faith renewed in messages sent
Alas, in dreams our homes' in sight
By yonder window's candlelight.

June 16, 2003

Blessed Assurance

"So them, so is land, even was moved, it yet shall ye be"

The Lord moves heaven and earth, and so shall ye be moved. Though firm in stance on issues important to man, God's holy plan demands that we too are moved; according to His will and compassion.

Just as catastrophic events move mountains and spread burning flames across the wilderness, so shall our worlds be placed in turmoil and chaos, accordingly. The days of peace and quiet will surely return at which time we must reflect upon our blessings and that which we hold most dearly in our hearts: our faith in God.

"Blessed assurance" is the comfort to be found in one's faith. Not constant protection from the ills of this world at this place and time; but the eternal peace and salvation from our sins, to be found in the comfort of His Word. Through Jesus Christ, our Savior, now and forever more

Amen

July 3, 2003

When Thou Shalt Harken

"When thou shalt harken to the voice of the Lord thy God, to keep all his commandments which I command thee this day, to do *that which is* right in the eyes of the Lord thy God."

Deuteronomy 13:18

What a powerful verse; timely for all generations, clearly and concisely stated, and most of all affirmative. *To do that which is* leaves no ambiguities; no questions and no doubts for the measure of performance is *in the eyes of the Lord*, the One who knows all and sees all; the same who not only gave us commandments, but commands us *this day*.

Dear Lord, may we never forget or underestimate the wisdom of thy word. Written down in stone but intended for the loving hearts of men and women, may we embrace thy commandments in word and deed.

With a thirst for understanding, at the well of knowledge to be found in the Good Book, may we develop in us the will and strength of character of those who have traveled before us. Your Son, our Lord and Savior walked with the disciples among the masses in distant lands. And yet, today the journey continues with each breath we take each hand we hold, every word we speak and every heart enjoined.

Blessed be the Word of God.

July 11, 2003

Before the Cock Crows

There is a special peace and quiet in the early morn on a country farm. Before the cock crows, many farmers are up and about, before the break of dawn and rising temperatures. Unlike those who have short commutes to work in offices, stores or warehouses, a farmer's commute begins and ends at his kitchen door.

When the disciples walked with Jesus, I would not doubt that many of their travels occurred in the cool evenings or before the break of dawn. And such is true for us today. For you see, the dawn of salvation begins when we come to know the wisdom of the word. When Jesus foretold Peter "The cock shall not crow until thou hast denied me thrice" Peter was still living in darkness; even though he claimed to be willing to lay down his life for Jesus. Not until the day of salvation, when Jesus was accused and Peter was confronted three times, did the dawn of salvation become apparent to Peter.

We too are waiting the day of salvation, and like Peter we are likely to deny the mist that clouds our judgment; question the advice that we actually long to hear: the truth and Christ's blessing.

Just before Jesus rebuked Peter's pledge to defend Jesus issues one last, all important, commandment. Knowing that his disciples still were living in darkness, and that the dawn of salvation was soon at hand, Jesus says: "A new commandment I give unto you, That ye love one another; as I have loved you, that ye also love one another. By this shall all men know that ye are my disciples, if ye have love one to another."

Go forth this day, my friends, in the comfort and knowledge that by living according to this commandment thou shalt know one another in spite of the darkness that shall one day end with the dawn of salvation.

John 13:37 & 38
John 13:34 &35

July 12, 2003

In the Midst of His Temple

Seeking what is right before ones eyes without question or concern for that which one might dread

In the midst of His temple there is a comfort to be discovered.
From the beauty of a soft morning sunrise over the Atlantic, to the gentle lighting of a butterfly on a seashell's edge; such is the wonder of faith, the peace of solace and the pleasure of His love.

No temple ever built by the hand of man can compare with that which surrounds us every day.
From the blueprints of creation recorded in Genesis, to the foundation of the world placed in firmament.
The reckoning of wonders to behold from the distant galaxies to the smallest identified elements that make up, or matter ... His is the tabernacle of the eternal grace, endless marvel and eternal faith.

In the midst of His temple there is peace.

July 27, 2003

"We have thought of thy loving kindness, O God, in the midst of thy temple."

Psalm 48:9

A City of Truth

In Zechariah 8 the beauty of a city of truth is foretold. The Lord of hosts tells us of a wrath that shall be spared and of how one's hands must be strong ye that hear in these days these words by the mouths of the prophets.

Strength can be developed or found by many means. And there are many strengths: strength of will, strength of character, a strong heart; but here, the Lord of hosts references letting your hands be strong. It is often said that actions speak louder than words, as does this passage. For in the next verse 10, "For before these days there was no hire for man nor hire for any beast . . ." Idle hands prevailed as "neither *was there any peace* to him that went out or came because of the affliction . . ."

The possibilities of a city of truth begin with strong hands whose actions lay the foundation. The best intentions do not lift a single stone; but if we follow what the Lord of hosts says in Zechariah 8:16 & 17 and "Speak ye every man the truth to his neighbour; execute the judgment of truth and peace in your gates . . ." these are the things that we shall do. The foundation of which lies in our strong hands and what we do. What we speak is liken to the mortar that sets quickly the stone; be it the foundation of faith or cornerstone of justice; the course is set by truth.

July 27, 2003
Zechariah 8:9-10

De"scribing" the Naysayer

In the book of Mark, Chapter 2, the use of words common to today are juxtaposed with the miracles that are uncommon to any other man, but Jesus. I call your attention to words like "press" and "scribes" . . . "fashion" and "resorted" . . . and "receipt of custom"

Today we refer to the media as the press, and just as "when they could not come nigh unto him **but for the press**, they uncovered the roof where he was." (4) Today, wherever crowds are gathered, thereto one will find the press; to uncover the story within.

The final line in verse 12, after Jesus heals the ill, the amazed crowd praises God and declares: "'We never saw it **on this fashion**." Later, in verse 21, Jesus refers to the parable of how **"No man seweth a piece of new cloth on old garment."** What is fashion today, if it not be a new design, new fabrics . . . or a "new cloth."

In verse 13, Jesus "went forth again **by the sea side;** and all the multitude **resorted** unto him." Is it no small matter that today's greatest resorts, and source of peace and personal restoration are often found at the sea sides.

"And as he passed by he saw Levi, son of Alphaeus, sitting **at the receipt of custom."** Later on in verse 22, Jesus refers to the parable of **"No man putteth new wine into old bottles."** Today, travelers purchase new wines in custom shops, where neighbors meet and people must pass by.

The translations of the original books of the bible fascinate me as many were translated from Greek, Hebrew, and Latin. But what I enjoy most is how these words and phrases, even when translated into English, are so timeless in their ability to convey the word of the God. How the messages foretell, and are followed by examples that are still appropriate today.

Just as the disciples spoke in many tongues, the ongoing interpretations and meanings of the message of God through Christ continues today; easily understood and deeply appreciated.

When next you read a verse, or hear a story of Christ, look to the words, phrases and parables a little deeper. For what you'll discover, de"**scribes**" what the naysayer would want you to doubt, and opens your heart to a greater understanding of the love of God through Jesus (read Mark 6,7 & 8)

August 7, 2003

The Surety of the Shoe

The confirmation of commitments is an interesting phenomenon. With the clear intention of securing collateral of some form, many cultures and generations devised methods with interesting consequences. In the short book of Ruth, the Old Testament recounts the purchase of property, in which a kinsman, Boaz, offers surety for the purchase of land in a unique action.

"Now this was the manner in former time in Israel concerning redeeming and concerning changing, for to confirm all things; a man plucked off his shoe, and gave it to his neighbor: and this was a testimony in Israel." (Ruth 4:7)

Now consider, if you will, the importance of such an action whereby a man without one shoe is likened to a bicycle with only one wheel. As a surety, the shoe is given to a neighbor which in and of itself is an action of intent; for the surety giver knows where his shoe may be found, and the neighbor knows of the bargain, and will not return it until the transaction is closed. The phrase: "my brother's (or, in this case, neighbor's) keeper" somehow comes to mind here.

A confusing reference to "inheritance" ensues between Boaz and an unnamed kinsman of whom Boaz "spoke came by" (4.1). Now, Naomi was to sell a parcel of land that was their brother's, Elimelech. This reference suggests that a relationship might have existed between Naomi and Boaz; i.e. perhaps brother-in-law or cousin-in-law; hence, the question of inheritance.

Subsequently, Boaz takes Ruth as his wife, and she is blessed with a child who is nursed by Naomi, and called upon to be her child. "And the women said unto Naomi, Blessed be the Lord, which hath not left thee this day without a kinsman, that his name may be famous in Israel." (4:14) His name was Obed; and, although his father was

Boaz, his mother became Naomi through the loving kindness of her daughter-in-law, Ruth. In the last verse (4:22) "And Obed begat Jesse, and Jesse begat David" so that his name may be famous in Israel.

The importance of honoring a commitment is evident here as the very birth of David might not have occurred for the want of a shoe. The surety of the shoe's return completed a commitment, and by such action, the wheels were put into motion through love, trust and community values.

To walk with only one shoe, one risks permanent damage to oneself; and to walk with no shoes you can rest assured that the journey of life will be long and hard. But to fulfill one's obligations, the return of faith through action, will be a surety to the believer and a benefit to all.

As evidenced here in the short Book of Ruth, may your steps in life be assured in the return of favors and commitments to the Father, Son and Holy Spirit, Amen.

August 31, 2003

The Prayers of Thy Servants

Early mornings can be more difficult on some days more so than other days. The first day of work or school after a long vacation or short holiday can be a challenge both mentally and physically. Routines that once prevailed are broken, all but for a short time; and must be resurrected once again on the morning of the first day back. I recall one such humorous Monday morning as a young child:

My brothers and I would rise before the sun and after a quick breakfast of tea and toast, we would walk a half mile or so to the bus stop in front of our grand parents' home. There we would join a few other friends, and, as was the custom, either reflected on the past events of the holiday or were left to catch a few more minutes rest with our eyes closed tight.

This one particular morning I was the one in dire need of additional rest; and, as I stood there like a statue in the snow, my brother and neighbor joked out loud to my dismay. Well, I tried to ignore them, but as they toned down their voices into whispers, my ears drifted toward their conversation until I blurted out: "What did you say? What did you say? I wasn't looking!"

Well they both broke out in laughter as I realized the stupidity of my comment and how I had been sucked into their conversation subconsciously.

In the Book of Nehemiah, a similar verse that struck me as odd occurred as Nehemiah prayed in verse 6. Here he asks of God: ***"Let thine ear now be attentive, and thine eyes open, that thou may hearest the prayer of thy servant, which I pray before thee day and night."***

When seeking the attention of others it is as important to make eye contact as it is to speak loudly enough to be heard. The power of vision has become such an important medium that today's attempts to gain your attention must include some form of visual element. Even the cell phone has evolved to not only include graphic elements such as text (messaging) and photos, but can even transmit those to whomever you are speaking.

In prayer we often seek the same of our Lord. It is not enough that our words be sincere and from the heart, but we often seek a visual representation through our deeds, work and yes, even our writings, as I am doing so here now.

In the First Book of Kings, chapter 8, Verse 29, "That thine eyes may be open toward this house night and day . . ." Solomon's blessing toward the people seeks the oversight of our Lord, in addition to an attentive ear toward their prayers.

Just as I stood there half asleep at the school bus stop, we too are often half attentive to that which goes on around us every day. While waiting for our journey into Christ's word to begin, we are often blind to the ills of the world that herald before us, and deaf to the warning messages of others. Not until we are truly awakened can we combine the sights with the sounds and confirm that which has been true all along.

Such is the message of the Lord in both the Old and New Testaments. The word of God was often confirmed through visions: of a burning bush, of the Ten Commandments in stone, of salvation from the pharaohs and a miraculous birth unto the Virgin Mary. The restoration of healing until sinners and the resurrection of our Lord and Savior from the cross; all enlightened the Word through vision.

Today, when I return from a vacation or holiday, I pray that my ears may be attuned to the sights and sounds that surround me. For although our routines may have been broken, we must seek to break any routine that deafens our ears, or clouds our eyes, from the blessings of the God, set before us. May we awaken once more and confirm our faith that He is both listening and watching over, the prayers of the servants.

Amen

September 2, 2003

God's Call to Repentance

In Jeremiah 7, God's call to repentance is described by Jeremiah as he is to stand in the gate of the Lord's house.

"Amend your ways and your doings, and I cause you to dwell in this place." At first blush it appears that Jeremiah is referring to the Temple of the Lord; but in the next verse repeats three times the phrase: "Trust ye not in lying words, saying, The Temple of the Lord, The Temple of the Lord, The Temple of the Lord, are these."

The words of man in the house of the Lord carry not merit; for beyond the gate in our daily lives is where our actions speak the truth [Read verses 5-7]. For in verse 8, Jeremiah reveals "Behold ye trust in lying words that cannot profit."

Jeremiah asks those to come before him and stand and say: "We are delivered to do all these abominations?" The question is just for it confirms our confusion which suggests that we think that we are free of sin and do not understand[1] why this must be; here again we try to deny our own faults. But in verse 19, "Do they provoke me to anger?" saith the Lord; and the question is answered with a question: "do they not provoke themselves to the confusion of their own faces?"

If one believes in "free will," I mean truly believes in free will, would they ever be confused? A free will thinker makes a choice, an event follows and the results are understood and accepted for what they are. An abbreviation of freedom, free would mean without doubt, guilt or fear of consequence; an acceptance free of doubt.

In the scientific community there is a quest to achieve "absolute zero," in temperature, that is. No movement of molecules. Cold enough to a point where one cannot achieve even a fraction of a point or degree less.

I recall a winter when my wife and I traveled to see my brother and his new family outside of Chicago. We marveled at the beauty and contrast of towering skyscrapers against the fury of the elements in The Windy City. The contrast of one's senses, the desire to see the sights, and yet having to fight the elements reminded one of how good it was to be alive.

This particular winter season, record low temperatures were being approached; as the mercury pushed into double digit degrees below zero. While bundling layers upon layers of clothes we laughed at how futile it seemed to add any more layers since we wouldn't be able to move in any event (be it frozen or the stiffness of our mummy like wrappings). And the cars heaters were a joke as the windows frosted over with each breath we took. To our amazement, my young nephew and I would etch patterns into the frosty windows and puff over them as our breaths would freeze in layers.

The funny thing was, after reaching a certain temperature, perhaps 20 or 25 degrees below zero, it almost didn't matter, as you couldn't tell the difference at 30 or 35 degrees below! When I look back at this journey, it occurred to me as to why this may have been so: because here in the freezing cold, an "inner warmth" was growing within each of us. This was a special time with our first nephew, my wife and my brother with his wife, as we were all young and starting out on new lives. Like pioneers on the western plains, we were together; circling the wagons against the weather. As close to absolute zero, in terms of both temperature and personal wealth as we had ever been, we were young and glad to be in the comfort of His love. Not knowing what lied ahead, but thankful to be where we were, together.

Much has happened since that journey to Chicago. Another child followed and my wife and I had our own son. Many cities, jobs, happy and sad events have ensued. And if I chose to do so, I could be confused by it all; and, ask "why" we are delivered to all these abominations that occurred since those innocent days of our youth.

If I truly believed in free will and would accept without question or doubt, I fear that I would be approaching absolute zero: cold, uncaring, in different and . . . un-Christian.

"Trust ye not in lying words" for words can be as cold as absolute zero if they fail to speak with any emotion in the heart or soul. Just as we can never come close to the compassion and love shown to us by our Lord and Savior, Jesus, there is no free will for the born again Christian who has come to understand and appreciate the debt of salvation we owe to our good Shepard. The blood of Christ is on our hands. His is the only free will that has ever conquered the coldest depths of Hell, and now stands in the gate to our Lords house to shelter us from the cold for all eternity.

This is where our will resides; at the foot of Calvary, many years ago; and today, to be found in the warmth of His love shown to us through those we love.

Amen

September 22, 2003

Mist of Mine Eyes

May the mist of my eyes, now give way
For the sun of a new morning day
From whence all His blessings do flow
On this day, now in peace, I must go.

Wet these fingers mine eyes
I might see
Of thy gift now in sight
There might be
For the faith that I sought
Now is true
In the blessings of Christ
Found in you

Just as Jesus gave sight to the blind
In a mission of mercy, we find
That the faithful who followed where few
Spreads now broad as the sweet morning dew.

October 2, 2003

In Search of Peace

You share their goals, but not their methods,
These mighty men of war
In marches walked on foreign soils
To settle but a score

The roads diverge on native land
In search of peace we stand
As so do they, do not dismay
The way they chose, I pray

For marches here are just as clear
As on homeland grassy grounds
But the silence here is not so dear
When the bag pipes' dirge is sound

So send a prayer to those abroad
And to the enemies they meet
For when back to home they're bound,
May be the only sound
. . . a welcomed heart to greet.

October 7, 2003

A Pioneer's Prayer

Rising sun at one's back, setting moon up ahead
For each year that is past, is a burden we dread
That one ruleth by day and one ruleth by night
Through eyes the Almighty, sees He all that is right

No fear in this morning, on this journey set out
His love and compassion, leaves no reason for doubt
And each mile left behind, we'll revisit in time
With trust and the glory, Christ assures we will find

Place your faith in His hands, and your love in His heart
Together we'll treasure, on this day as we start
Heading west with the sun, and the moon as our guide
The Lord will be with us, 'til the day we arrive.

Amen

Psalm 136:8&9 and Psalm 139:12

October 14, 2003

Duty & The Golden Rule

"So likewise ye, when ye shall have done all those things which are commanded you, say, We are unprofitable servants: we have done that which was our **duty** to do."

Luke 17: 10

Duty. As an acronym, I think of it as you would "**do unto** yourself." For of the Ten Commandments, what would commandment would you not want others to honor in dealing with you? This is duty.

The commonly referenced "golden rule" suggests that one would profit in wealth by treating others as they would like to be treated; however, Luke 17 verse 10 our Lord and Savior confirms otherwise. That the "gold-in-rule" is the honor of fulfilling one's duty. Not profit, but servitude.

October 19, 2003

The Shittim Wood

How deep the grain of the shittim wood
Of character, beauty in life one should
Behold the colors that are rich hue
The miracle of nature found in me and you

Rare is its bounty and treasured for its looks
From the Ark of the Covenant to tabernacle roofs
Be it brazen alter or supporting polls
The shittim wood traversed distance shoals,

Be it wilderness cedar or gentle myrtle
In the desert sand or in soil fertile
Lo' the cedar tree, fir or pine together
Lest the shittah tree be the greatest treasure.

November 7, 2003

Always on Watch

These are the days when a war rages between those who seek peace and those who wage terror. A terror intended to cause nations to rise against nations, out of fear; when those seeking to deceive and many shall come. In the book of Mark, Chapter 13 verse 7, Jesus recounts "And when ye shall hear of wars and rumours of war, be ye not troubled: for such things must needs be, but the end shall not be yet."

Nature abounds with messages of where we are and what will come. Be it as simple as the moss on the north side of a tree or as complicated as the solar flares that we have come to understand will disrupt communications, signs of where we are or what will come abounds. Jesus instructs us to learn the parable of the fig tree: "When her branch is yet tender, and putteth forth leaves, ye know that summer is near." Here we are instructed to pray. For unlike the signs that abound in nature, we have no idea of when our master will come. "But on that day and that hour, knoweth no man, no not the angels which are in heaven, neither the son, but the Father."

The final instructions Jesus tells us of how the son of man is like a man taking a far journey and informs his servants, and to every man his work, and commanded the porter to watch. For we know not when the master of the house will return. Not to be found sleeping, we are instructed to watch.

> All that was spoken was found to be true
> Of the miracles and blessings to be found within you
> You told us to watch and to diligently pray
> The truth to be found in all you would say
>
> Be it sorrows to share or these wars to be fought
> The message is true in all lessons you've taught
> Though the seasons are true and the message is clear
> Be we always on watch for our master is near.

November 24, 2003

Hide & Seek

To confide takes a special strength. Be it with a friend, a minister or priest, one's spouse or any other requires an exposure and display of vulnerability. It can be a difficult act for we have been taught to protect ourselves; to be reserved out of fear that what we confide in others could be used against us.

But what of the Lord? How difficult can it be to confess our sins to the One who knows everything? In the book of Job "Behold, I go forward, but he is not there; and backward, but I cannot perceive him: he hideth himself on the right hand, that I could not see him: but he knoweth the way that I take: when he hath tried me, I shall come forth as gold."

Just as Job seeks the Lord to debate and plead unto him, Job finds him not; but in the next line a confidence in His presence is confirmed:

"My foot hath held his steps, his way have I kept, and not deceived."

There is an enjoyable blues song by two performers known as Sonny & Brownie. In it, Brownie retells a story of how man and God play hide and seek. In the role of God, Sonny's background comments, to man's frustration at his foolishness is recounted after man gives up and builds himself an image which "brings him nothing but pain." Finally man discovers that God is right there inside of him. Having looked everywhere, on top of mountains and into the sea, man discovers that God is right there "inside of you and in me." Sonny confirms that, as God says "I'm everywhere, man."

The closing chorus of Sonny and Brownies' song about man and

God repeats: "God is in you and God is in me, and to love all of God is to love humanity."

Once exposed to the word of God and understanding a new confidence is secured; a confidence in God's mercy no matter what foolish self-serving paths and images we might chose to pursue. There is one truth and it is everywhere to be found in Christ and no where to be hidden, in you and in me.

November 24, 2003

Trailings

Trailings... have you ever enjoyed watching the vapor trails of jets as they crisscrossed the sky in the early evening sunset? The reflection of light and the patterns against a robin's egg blue background remind me of decorations found during one of our most treasured holidays, Easter. So often in life, the trailings of where we have been are a good indication of where we are, or the direction as to where we are headed. Just as we honor the memory of Jesus' resurrection, a sense of renewal with the welcome of another spring season assures us where we are in our Christian faith, born again.

After many years as a carpenter, Jesus' travels took him to many distant shores where he was so often welcomed, occasionally feared and frequently questioned. From a humble career working with wood, his teachings and parables often reflected upon nature and all its grandeurs. References to trees, vines and branches abound in the teachings as they portrayed our relationships with our Lord and each other. Such as the parable of the fig tree: "When her branch is yet tender, and putteth forth leaves, ye know that summer is near."

It is in these passages, where we come to appreciate the sincerity of His blessings, the treasure of His oratory skills and His genuine love for all mankind. Just as we learn of others throughout history, this wonderful book, the bible, has become a trailing of many lives for all to see and enjoy. By studying where prophets, disciples, and our Lord and Savior have been and what they have shared with others, a greater understanding of where we are and the destination that awaits us unfolds. Through the joy of discovery we see how events of today relate to the teachings of yesterday, and our bible, and the one word of God, becomes the center of one's universe.

Beyond our greatest understanding we can be secure in the knowledge that we are loved by One so gentle and kind. To wash away our sins and shelter us from harm here on earth through His promise of a greater life eternal, we can refocus on our journey once again, with a renewed spirit.

Dear Father, we thank you for the inspirations, understandings and assurances that we discover in following the lives of your Son, His disciples and the prophets before them as recounted throughout the bible. At a time and place where we may be fraught with fear and concerns over the events unfolding in our daily lives, may we continue to find rest and reassurance in the word of you, our God. During events of joy and happiness may we be humble in our prayers and adorations, giving thanks to thee from where all blessings flow. Thanks for the giving of a loving family. Thanks for the giving of shelter from the cold. Thanks for the giving of food for our health. And most importantly, thanks for the giving of your only Son, our Lord and Savior. Amen

November 27, 2003

Liberty

What is the sound of liberty? It is what calls us to gather in freedom and others to disperse under tyranny. **Liberty is not a sound, but a virtue. For the virtuous know that to counter the tyranny of oppression, one must respond with an equal or greater force of free will. Just as the Liberty Bell suspends at rest, attempts to dislodge or remove it occur, the weight of its power responds against the opposing force. Such is the spirit of freedom, and the virtue of our liberty. Our bell of liberty and freedom was rung many years ago, but its sound is as true today as it was in 1776, for those and all Americans who rely on its virtue.** The ability to gather together in peaceful protest, or to speak our minds and express our opinions in public, to select our leaders and remove our oppressors, such is the will of a free man and women.

Revere it for its beauty and strength, but respect it for its virtue. Protect it for the delicate balance which it must maintain to remain at rest. And know that although it is not perfect, as evidenced by the crack in its bronze casting, it will be an enduring symbol in the heart of everyone who has experienced the importance of freedom and the virtue of American liberty.

December 1, 2003

Seeing It Through, II

Seeing it through; such were the disciples Peter and John with their followers in their determination to do, as it is recounted in the Book of Acts, Chapter 4. Here, under confrontation and interrogations of elders and those of authority to the acts and miracles, that was performed in the name of Jesus of Nazareth.

When commanded to speak not to any man in the name of Jesus, Peter and John answered: "Whether it be right in the sight of God to hearken unto you more than unto God, judge ye. For we cannot but speak the things which we have seen and heard."

Last year I wrote of "seeing it through" with the following poem:

See It Through

>Speak not my lovely children
>With a bitterness in thy heart
>Hold back thy words in silence
>When you are about to start
>
>Down the road of unbridled vengeance
>Is a journey with no end in sight
>When one has the time or leisure
>To pray or prepare to fight
>
>In earnest self reflection
>Look deep within thy soul
>To know the will of destiny
>And fulfill one's sacred goal

Be it peaceful confrontation
Or a line drawn in the sand
If a war is unavoidable
Make a pledge and then take a stand

That no matter what course is chosen
Nor whatever deed thou do
Seek in prayer to a higher calling
In God's will you will see it through.

(September 6, 2002)

This is what Peter and John demonstrated: the ability to see it through, in spite of the will of man, and in honor of the glory of God. Throughout generations and the coming and going of nations, doctrines and the self serving authorities of mankind, one truth remains unblemished and unchallenged: the will of God. Peter and John knew this, the disciples and followers knew this, and even the elders and those of authority knew this. And now, even we know this, through the word of God.

December 1, 2003

A Child of God, and Children of His Works

In the Book of Luke, before the 4th chapter recounts the temptations of Christ by Satan, John the Baptist recounts the names of the fathers, or generations from Adam right on up to Joseph, the supposed father of Jesus. Throughout the recounting of fathers and sons, some names of familiarity surface, such as Simeon, Obed, Judah, Jacob, Jesse, Isaac and Seth; while others seem obscure or unfamiliar. Names like Jorim, Cosam, Melea and Saruch.

History recounts the names of famous people, or those we wish to honor, as remembered in the names that we pass on to our children. Sometimes they are names that are familiar to the masses for heroic deeds, while others are called according to the kindness that one has privately shown to another. But just as all were tempted by Satan, both before and after the coming of Jesus Christ, not all will acquiesce. For as many names known for the wonderful deeds that they have done in a lifetime, there are many others of the same name who have befallen to Satan's temptations.

In Chapter 3 of Luke, the most common verse reads: *"which was the son of."* Seventy five times, from Jesus, whose supposed father was Joseph, *which was the son of* Heli, the phrase *"which was the son of"* continues right up to Adam, *which was the son of* God. Seventy five generations, all of whom were tempted, many of whom were named after famous individuals (or, who were famous in their own rights) are recounted. But here, in the words of John the Baptist, we are told to "prepare ye the way of the Lord." Every year we do the same, as in the weeks between Thanksgiving and Christmas, when our thoughts and efforts are once again returned to prepare for the coming Jesus. Just as John forewarned, and the Lord confirmed as the Holy Ghost descended like a dove upon him, when Jesus was baptized, the Lord said "Thou are my beloved Son; in thee I am well pleased." Beloved son; from Adam whom God created, through generations of man until Jesus, the son of God arrived, John chronicles the heritage of man and the blessing of the Lord.

In verse 8, John calls on those to *"bring forth therefore fruits worthy of repentance, and begin not to say within yourselves, We have Abraham to our father: for I say unto you, That God is able of these stones to raise up children unto Abraham."* In these words, he differentiates man's belief in man and stresses our Creator above all men. But even those who heard his words looked to confirm man's greatness when in verse 15 it is written: *"And as the people were in expectation, and all men mused in their hearts of John, whether he were the Christ or not;"* John answered saying unto them all, *I indeed baptize you with water; but one mightier than I cometh . . ."* To confirm the humility in which we must acknowledge our Savior, John continues and says: *". . . the latchet of whose shoes I am not worthy to unloose."*

It is good to find pride and honor in the naming of our children, the remembrance of our fathers and others; but, it can never replace or disrespect the fact that they and we are only human; with faults, temptations and misgivings which can only be forgiven by Christ, our Lord and Savior. Let us remember this in our prayers, for that whom we await in this blessed season comes as a child is "the Son of God" and, we are but the children of His works.

December 6, 2003

For Those Low in Spirit

There are those low in spirit and sad of fate. For theirs is the sorrow born of illness, fear of the morrow and for what new ailments may beseech them. If I must join them, may my compassion not wane. If I can help them, may my will be strong. If I am now with them, may hands not delay. If this is my destiny may I welcome thy will; for thou art my Father, my Master in all that matters.

Without question, doubt or reservations, I shall wait on the Lord. For it is He who is was heralded by angels at birth, taught wisdom to the multitudes, spoke to heathens, healed illness and brought hope to all who believed . . . in our Lord and Savior.

Amen

December 11, 2003

Companions and Christ

A companion is a dear term. The declaration of a common bond or shared friendship can be born of various events. The camaraderie of a team effort, schoolyard chums, volunteer organization or shared plight can bring two or more souls together in a very special way.

In Hebrews 10, verses 32 to 37, the Lord calls on us to *remember the former days in which **after you were illuminated** ye endured a great fight of afflictions;* how true this is with knowledge and understanding. Upon discovery of a truth, it can be emotionally unnerving as you think, act and feel differently about your past, present and future

Such was the birth, life and death of Jesus Christ; for the illumination of our understanding of life through He who brought us together at His birth. And, through His life like *grazing stock by both reproaches and afflictions, whilst ye became companions of them that were so used.* Recall the sermons, proverbs and restoration of those afflicted.

34. For ye had compassion of me in my bonds, and took joyfully the spoiling of your goods, knowing in yourselves that ye have in heaven a better and enduring substance. Here, the confirmation of how we come to see how the sacrifice of one so pure and loving assures us that whatever of value we loose here on earth is nothing compared to the glory that awaits us in heaven.

In the next verse, we are told to *cast not away therefore your confidence which hath great recompense of reward. For ye yea have need of patience, that after ye have done the will of God, ye might receive the promise.* Confidence in the loss, that a greater gain (reward) awaits us; hence the need for patience, for which we might receive, as promised.

It all starts with companions, and that which brings us together: like a distant star, the heralding of angels and the alpha, our Savior.

Companions, compassion and confidence . . . all lead to patience and the promise of life everlasting, the omega, through Christ Jesus. Amen

December 17, 2003

Hero in the Heart

There's a hero in the heart,
of most every son and man
Who no matter what their start,
must one day take a stand
In the families' best interests,
and in all they know is right
Be it need that they apologize,
or prepare and engage the fight

As I look back on the life,
of the man I call my father
Now aware of all the strife,
bitter victories and bother
Would be easier to give up,
or walk on out the door
Be it not for his great love,
and compassion to do more

You have strengthened this, our family,
by the life that you have led
And faced the world's great evils,
and the problems that we dread
As all your sons are grateful,
for all that you may do
May the hero in our hearts,
reflect the grace we've found in you.

December 20, 2003

A Poem for my Father

Filled with Prayers and Wishes

Two bottles for that what ails you,
Who deserves all the best of life
Keep them close now by your bedside
To protect you through the night

One the *Nectar of The Golden Life*:
That is *Health and Vitality*
The other *Ball and Claw of Bitters*
For what must surely be temporary

For though these now seem empty
It is because of all that you have given
To others who are ever grateful
For the wonderful life you're living

So don't think these are merely empty
Filled with what you cannot see
It's the love and prayers we're sending
For God's grace and love in thee

December 20, 2003

        A Poem for my Mother

The Seal is Broken . . .

But the Contents Are Safe

In ancient days the use of seals was common, be it the storehouse to the Pharaoh's grains, a message carried by a courier to distant monarchs or the tombs of great kings. Today as we look upon the great architectural wonders of the world, many are weather worn and broken, and yet they still hold many mysteries to be uncovered.

Such is the fate of man, who in his greatest hour of prominence has the attention of all who surround him, be it in life or in death. Regardless of one's station in life, that which is within you has the potential to impact on the lives of those around you. Like the contents, before the seal is broken, what is within us is often unknown. But once the seal is broken, wonders and mysteries from within can have a profound effect on all who are blessed with the discovery.

Throughout history, albeit ancient times or today's news, seals are being broken and discoveries are changing the very world around us, everyday. Seals of deceit, be it corporate malfeasance or unearthed mass graves. Seals of success, like the 100th year anniversary of the Wright brothers' first flight, and seals of compassion, like the news of an unmarried soldier giving his lottery won holiday leave from Iraq to his friend, the father of a seven year old boy. There are seals on letters carrying holiday greetings to friends and loved ones and sealed gifts being opened every day during these glorious holidays. And yet, in each instance, as the seals are broken, we look to find the contents within, hopefully safe and undamaged.

The key here is this: to discover the contents' condition and potential value, a seal must be broken. The act requires an effort, and the effort requires a commitment, and the commitment requires a faith. A faith that what you believe, can only be confirmed by an action; hence, a circle which can only be entered if you so chose. Wherever, or however is immaterial . . . but you must break into the seal of the circle. But what you will discover is not always what you might expect.

The three wise men saw a star and set out to find a king. With sealed gifts in hand they brought that which would be valued by a king in a palace surrounded by wealth and finery; protected by soldiers and dignitaries. But what they discovered was a child in manger, surrounded by beasts and shepherds. And yet, their discovery of a king was confirmed. Content* with the truth that they discovered, a sacred bond to return by another route sealed the protection of that which they had discovered. For there are those in life who will attempt to destroy the truth.

Content and contentment are interesting words. Synonyms for the word "contentment" include: satisfaction, happiness, pleasure, gratification and ease. If the truth within us be known, the **contents** of our lives were **meant** to be these very terms: satisfying, happy, enjoyable and rewarding. This year when you open your holiday cards, gifts and doors to visitors, may the contents that you discover bring you the joy and happiness as it was meant to be. May they break the seal on your heart with the spirit of Christmas, so that you too, may find Peace on Earth.

Amen

December 21, 2003

Peace on Earth

Listen to the tinkle
Of bells in distant lands
Watching shoppers wander
With gifts and smiles in hand

Voices singing carols
Of wonders to be found
While mistletoe and holly
In boughs of wreath abound

The aroma of an evergreen
With bright lights within the tree
Brings out the joy and happiness
Of that child in you and me.

Though Christmas past and memories
Fade with the aging years
The life of one, so Holy
Dispels our sorrows, pains and fears.

For peace on earth is possible
When you welcome from the heart
On this Christmas Day of blessings
'Til the day we must depart.

'Tis the season when a child
In Bethlehem that night
Brought peace on earth to man
And the word to set it right

December 24, 2003

A Faithful Crossing

It was a dreary wet day as I traveled west on Washington, just east of Nassau Street. The crosswalk up ahead had four pedestrians under two umbrellas waiting for a break in the flow of traffic. Approaching the group, I slowed to a stop while signaling them on to safely cross. The couple that was nearest my car were young and clearly in love. As the young man held the umbrella in one hand, his other reached ever so tenderly behind the back of his companion. Next to them were two parents, fairly senior in years, but obviously young in heart. All were well dressed and enjoying their time together on this blustery day before Christmas.

Under the other umbrella, the lady held their cover from the rain out in front and between them as the shaking white haired man smiled and held her other hand ever so gratefully following her lead into the street. It occurred to me, at that moment, as I thought about our son, his girlfriend, my wife and I, how time can reverse all roles. But when love is close in hand, and faith is a sure hand to escort and protect, hope will be the guiding heart that leads.

Regardless of the weather, health, wealth or circumstances, faith hope and love will protect the kindred spirit. And our crossing will not be a journey taken alone, nor ever in vain.

December 24, 2004

Index

A

Aaron 90
Acts 215, 218, 223
Acts 4 348
Acts 9
  26-39 219
Adam 289

B

Bartimaeus 188
Book of Ruth 330

C

Christmas 132, 264
Corinthians 228
Corinthians 13 229
CORINTHIANS 9
  11 242
Corinthians II 235
Corinthians II, 4
  8 239
Corinthians II, 6 237

D

Daniel 10
  24 168
Deuteronomy 13:18 322

E

Easter 304
Elisabeth 305
Epistle to Ephesians 248
Epistle to Titus 1
  7-9 273
Eve 289

F

First Book of Kings, 8
  29 332

G

Galatians 2
  2 243
Genesis 291
Genesis 19:1-11 293
Genesis 4
  20 289
Genesis, Chapter 48 13-21 298
Genesis Chapter 50, verse 20 302

H

Hebrews 10 353
Hebrews 9 277
  16 & 17 277
  28 277
HOSEA 10
  12 159

J

Jacob 90, 298
Jeremiah 7 333
Jesus 16, 53, 66, 74, 95, 108, 116, 124, 145, 147, 164, 166, 169, 172, 174, 176, 182, 188, 192, 194, 201, 203, 204, 212, 215, 216, 219, 223, 226, 231, 236, 251, 259, 264, 285, 287, 291, 296, 304, 308, 310, 312, 314, 315, 323, 327, 335, 336, 341, 348, 351, 353
Job 343

John 54, 169, 176
John 12
  24 209
John 13 324
John 15
  12,13 211
John 16
  2,3 212
John the Baptist 195, 305, 350
Joseph 298

L

Lot 293
Luke 194
Luke 1 & 2 192
Luke 1: 5763 305
Luke 12
  48 197
Luke 17
  10 339
Luke 22
  32 203
Luke 23
  28 & 31 204
Luke 23:12 312
Luke 3 350
Luke 3 verses 4 & 22 317
Luke 4
  1-13 307

M

Malachi 3
  1 168
Mark 192, 194
Mark 13
  2,8,10,11,12 190
  7 341
Mark 16 191
Mark 3
  3 182
Mark 9
  47 187
Mark, chapter 10 188
Mark Chapter 2 327

Matthew 11
  28-30 172
Matthew 13 174
Matthew 14 176
Matthew 18
  18 104
Matthew 27 179
Matthew 3
  1,2 169
Matthew 9 16, 278
Matthew 9:36-38 76
Moses 90, 98, 287

N

Nehemiah 6 331
Noah 291, 296

P

Paul 70, 145, 150, 206, 223, 225, 229,
      230, 235, 237, 239, 243, 248, 273
Peace 90, 94, 126
peace 48, 52, 67, 68, 71, 82, 86, 98,
      103, 113, 119, 127, 133, 141, 143,
      144, 145, 155, 161, 171, 175, 179,
      180, 181
Peter 90, 177, 204, 215
Philip 218
Proverbs 17
  6 90
Proverbs 22
  2 64
Psalm 136
  8&9 338
Psalm 139
  12 338
Psalm 48
  9 325
Psalm 62, verse 9 318
Psalms 54, 79

R

Romans 225

Z

Zacharias 305
Zechariah 12
  10 168
Zechariah 14
  4 168
Zechariah 8 326

www.ingramcontent.com/pod-product-compliance
Lightning Source LLC
Chambersburg PA
CBHW032059090426
42743CB00007B/174